The
SOCCER
GOALKEEPER

The Complete Practical Guide
for Goalkeepers and Coaches

Library of Congress Cataloging - in - Publication Data

by, Lawniczak, Jean-Marie and Puxel, Christian
  The Soccer Goalkeeper - The Complete Practical Guide for
  Goalkeepers and Coaches

ISBN # 1-890946-55-9
Library of Congress Catalog Number 00-191856
Copyright © October 2000

Art Direction/Layout
Kimberly N. Bender

Editing and Proofing
Bryan R. Beaver

Printed by
DATA REPRODUCTIONS
Auburn, Michigan

Cover Photography
EMPICS

REEDSWAIN Publishing
612 Pughtown Road
Spring City • Pennsylvania 19475
1-800-331-5191
www.reedswain.com
EMAIL: info@reedswain.com

The SOCCER GOALKEEPER

The Complete Practical Guide for Goalkeepers and Coaches

by
Christian Puxel
French National Team Goalkeeper Coach

Jean-Marie Lawniczak
French National Team Goalkeeping Coaches Academy Chairman

Published by
REEDSWAIN *Publishing*

PREFACE BY PHILIPPE BERGEROO

Philippe Bergeroo's career, in short:

- **Clubs Bordeaux, Lille, Toulouse.**
- **French National Team;**
- **Team manager, Assistant Manager in the French Team since 1994;**
- **Coaching the French team's goalkeepers since 1989.**
- **Regional Technical Adviser since 1992.**

Coaching the goalkeeper is a complicated process which involves education and coaching.

Coaching in itself has but one aim: the player must achieve a maximum result following specific means based on the following criteria:

- Developing physical and psychological skills and capacities,
- Coaching and improving the acquired knowledge,
- Acquiring the fundamentals of the game,

all of which will be the groundwork for a great future success.

Managing a coaching session is not an easy task.
It is, therefore, necessary to be fully aware of any potential difficulties which may arise, in order to acquire a perfect understanding of this particular subject.

This is why I insist that all coaches, educators and players, who are familiar with the game should express their thorough interest in this book, in order to extract all the potential it contains.

I sincerely congratulate the authors of this book; it brings precise and reliable answers to all situations of the game.

PREAMBLE BY J BATS

J Bats' career, in short:

- **Clubs of Sochaux, Auxerre, Paris Saint-Germain.**
- **French National Team from 1983 to 1989.**
- **European champion (1984).**
- **French champion (1986).**
- **World cup 1986- (3rd).**

Since the task of a modern goalkeeper is so important, it is essential to give him specific coaching.

Acquiring both the skills and trust are very important elements towards his success.

He will, therefore, need suitable exercises in order to face a large number of situations in the game.
The main interest will then be to link the exercises in order to acquire the ability to move from one situation to another.

I think that this book, written by C. PUXEL and J.M LAWNICZAK, is an excellent work tool, in quality as much as in the variety of exercises offered, even if no one can claim to possess the entire truth.

It is up to you to put things into perspective and fit the exercises in this book into introductory courses, improvement, and coaching, according to your specific needs and means.

Any amount of work requires demand and care. Nevertheless, **do not forget that, first and foremost, soccer remains a game.**

So, work with passion, try to pass it on and let it be shared so that coaching, particularly amongst the younger players, remains a pleasure and not a strain.

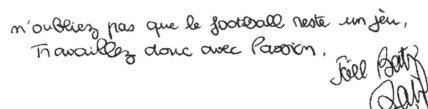

STEPS TOWARDS THIS GUIDE

Years of experience as players, coaches, educators and technical advisors in various clubs as well as specific coaching have led us to write this book.

As a starting point to personal research work and in order to take a new look at our pedagogical practice, this book is, first of all, a work tool for club coaches and goalkeepers.

We hope you will be able to handle the many facets of the position of goalkeeper in a better way.

Christian PUXEL and Jean-Marie LAWNICZAK

ACKNOWLEDGEMENTS

We would like to thank the people who have contributed to the drafting and completion of this book
In particular:
Gérard HOULLIER for his support
Nadine GERMAIN for her necessary steps and receptiveness
Romain CAILLER and Frédéric BOURGEAULT Goalkeepers
Anne BAUD for her drawings and advice
UHLSPORT for the equipment

LEGEND

 The ball

THE PLAYERS

Front/profile view

In Black = Goalkeeper
In Grey = Server of the balls (coach).

Aerial view

Goalkeeper or player

Opposite striker or screen player

Server of balls (coach) or neutral player

THE MOVES (goalkeepers and field players)

〜〜〜〜〜 Lateral side steps/backward dragging steps (fencing steps).

◀〜〜〜 Crossed steps (diagonal backward run).

〜〜〜▶ Running without the ball.

⊗〜〜〜▶ Running with the ball.

〜〜▶ Increase in the speed of movement.

TRAJECTORY OF THE BALL

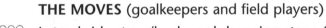 Direct aim and straight line.

In the air and lobbed.

VARIOUS

△ Cone	⊓ Bench
↓ Pole	 Mat
Fence	Mini-Trampoline
⬭ Hoop	Springboard
Magnifying glass	Forward/backward rotation

EMPHASIS (points to success)

✳✳✳ = Essential remarks or corrections.

✳✳ = Very important remarks or corrections.

✳ = Important remarks or corrections.

CHAPTERS

METHODOLOGY

Two main fields
Physical Coaching
Technical Preparation

METHODOLOGY

FOREWORD

This guide will enable you to discover the two main fields which characterize the goalkeeper's practice, i.e.:

- **physical training**
- **technical training**

Two **different topics** will be tackled within these two fields:

They will be divided into **two main themes** within which we will set out to discern **three coaching standards**:

- **Introductory coaching** (8-12 year olds)
- **Improvement which includes coaching** 12-15 year olds
  and coaching 16-21 year olds
- **Advanced coaching** (21 years old and above)

Each level will provide **suitable and progressive game situations** (250 exercises and 25 specific games).

The **original aspects** of this guide **highlight** the characteristics of each movement. These **points to success** will enable you to analyze in order to **alter** or **reinforce** the goalkeeper's technique.

SUMMARY STATEMENT

	INTRODUCTION	IMPROVEMENT		COACHING
	8-12 years old	Pre-Coaching 12-15 years old	Coaching 16-21 years old	Seniors 16-21 +21 years old
PHYSICAL	**Slow Motion Exercises**	**IN MOTION**		**Combining speed of the game + Basic techniques**
	Psycho-motivation (without the ball)	**INTRODUCING THE BALL**		
TECHNIQUE	**Quality of the movements (breakup the movements)**	**Quality in a game situation**	**Quality in the intensity of the game**	
	From a standstill position to a move	**IN MOTION**		**Adapt to the speed of the game**
	Exercise without Opposition	**Moderate Opposition**	**Dynamic Opposition**	**Opposition as in a real game (aggressiveness)**

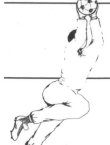

PRINCIPLES OF ACTION

In order to be sure that all the situations of the game are correctly applied, the coach must take into account a certain number of **pedagogical principles which cannot be ignored:**

- Estimate the level of your goalkeepers in order to i**dentify the exercises** which will correspond to each individual, i.e.: a 15 year old may find himself in an introductory coaching session on clearance.

You will thus work out the **levels of capability** specific to each goalkeeper.

- **Adapt to** their physical and mental state during each session and, as regards to the improvement in their movements, **be patient**. You must, therefore, avoid situations in which they will remain at a standstill or be cut off and do not hesitate to vary from one standard to another.

Insist on the **corrective** which corresponds to the **prevailing subject** of study. Indeed, the same exercise may be carried out following different themes. It is up to you to **stress exclusively** the aspects of the exercise which need to be **highlighted**.

Finally, the coaching session must take into account the **morphology** of each goalkeeper and **the physiological principles** which correspond to the different phases of his coaching.
You must therefore **adapt to the intensity** of the exercises and **vary the length or the number of repetitions and include** suitable **resting periods**.

VALUES AND COACHING SPIRIT

This original setup will allow each individual coach to **classify the appropriate exercises** to each of his coaching sessions.

You must therefore:

- **Draft a report on the deficiencies of activity** of your goalkeepers after several matches and coaching sessions.

- **Draw up a number of progressive exercises**, taking into account the number of goalkeepers who are at your disposal during the coaching session.

- **Repeat a large number of performances** in a very short period of time (repetition: every 7 seconds minimum) to help your players memorize the movements.

In all situations the goalkeeper **must not put up with half measures.** Therefore, as soon as the coaching period is over, it is essential to **expand his "100% goalkeeper's mentality"**. He will then carry out each action perfectly and at maximum speed.

PHYSICAL
PREPARATION

THE MOVES

In modern soccer several factors (heavy topspin, a wet ball. . .) can present difficulties for the goalkeeper.

Indeed, whatever the quality of his reflex and his impulse, there are always situations which are beyond his control.

In order to face up to these situations, he must, in all circumstances, begin each action with a movement which he will need to adapt to the different trajectories of the ball.

We will therefore study the following movements:

LATERAL MOVEMENTS
side stepping

INTRODUCTION

Objectives The goalkeeper moves laterally, without crossing his legs (side-stepping) towards a ball which is thrown close to him (maximum: 5 yards) still facing the game.

Organization Mark the area of the move (10 yards square) with 2 cones, then carry out the exercise within the goal area.

1st situation Between two cones, a goalkeeper moves slowly without a ball from one cone to the other, arms at his sides then forearms horizontal (mime the catch of the ball).
Look for the quality of the movement

2nd situation Identical to the first with a ball held with both hands (forearms horizontal).

3rd situation Two goalkeepers facing each other exchange balls while moving (distance between the two about 3 yards).

4th situation The goalkeeper moves in the goal area from one post to the other; the ball is thrown from right to left by a server standing 6 yards from the goal area.

Hand-throw the ball then kick:
• on the ground
• half way
• high up in the air

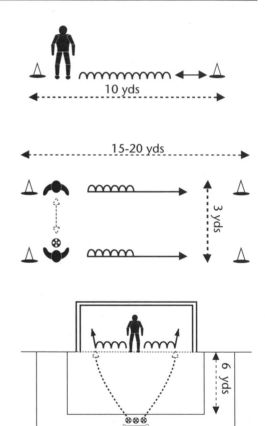

IMPORTANT!!!

The following steps must be used for all exercises:

1. Dragging steps (throwing the ball at shoulder level)

2. Bouncing steps (throwing the ball above the head)
    NOTE: use the dragging steps in order to place the body on the trajectory of the ball and bouncing steps to catch the ball.

3. Repeat the exercise right and left.

EMPHASIS (points to success)

With all movements preceding the catching of the ball, steps must be short and dragging (suspension period will be limited during the movement because the goalkeeper cannot act without ground support).

Use bouncing steps to catch a slow, high ball.

Weight must always be on the soles of the feet (heels off the ground).

Legs bent.

Straight torso.

Forearms horizontal (no arm swinging).

Keep an eye on the ball (avoid bending the head).

Limit the range of the first step; this will help find a good position on the trajectory of the ball.

II IMPROVEMENT

Objective   Quick sequential moves (catching the ball or diving) with or without moderate opposition.

Organization   Carry out the exercises between two cones, then in a real goal area.

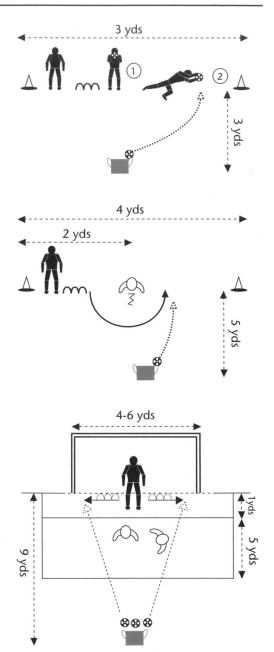

1st situation   A goalkeeper in the goal area.
A server at 3 yds throws the ball (alternating right and left).
The goalkeeper moves quickly:

1st step   Catching of ball – slow kick – (on the ground, hip high, high up)

2nd step   Dive for a ball - fast and distant kick – (begin with slanting steps - two steps then one or cross-steps before the dive to the ground) – See previous chapter.

N.B.   In this case, the goal area must be extended. (from 3 to 5 yds).

2nd situation   Identical to the 1st situation with moderate opposition.
The goalkeeper moves and catches the ball while avoiding an opponent at a standstill or in slow motion (passing in front of the opponent)

3rd situation   In a goal area, 4 by 6 yds, a goalkeeper moves in a lane 1 yd wide. In front of him, in the 6 yd area, one or two opponents stand as screens. The goalkeeper remains in his lane and must intercept all throws and kicks of the ball.
a) The "screen" striker or strikers do not touch the ball.
b) The striker or strikers can move and deflect the ball

EMPHASIS (points to success)

✳ Increase the speed of movement
✳✳ Teach the goalkeeper how to think ahead.

III PRACTICE

Objective Systematic combinations of side moves with various technical basic movements (catching of the ball or diving) as in a real game and including dynamic opponents.

Organization Exercise to be carried out in the goal area. Using a server as starter of the exercise is optional.

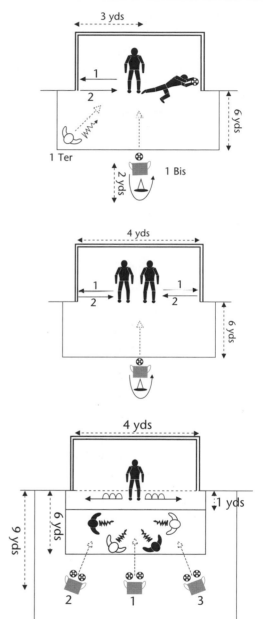

1st situation The goalkeeper begins his movement 3 yds from one of the goal posts.
He moves towards that post, touches it and returns to his initial position in order to intercept a ball or dive for a shot in the middle of the goal. The exercise is to be carried out to the right then to the left of the goal.

Variation 1 The server can become starter and begin the exercise by running around a block and back, to kick.

Variation 2 The server follows his kick and catches the ball which has been released by the goalkeeper (another striker can also be included).

2nd situation Identical to the first with one goalkeeper against another.
Each goalkeeper touches his own post.

Variations See 1st situation.

3rd situation Up to three servers at 9 yds from the goal, in the axis or on the sides:
In the 6 yd area, match two against two. The goalkeeper can only intercede in the one yd lane within the 6 yds area. (lateral sidestep). The strikers are banned from the lane.
Alternate the servers of the balls.

EMPHASIS (points to success)

✳ Carry out the above situations as in a real game (game intensity).

✳ ✳ Use the appropriate movements towards a stop reflex or a dive at the legs.
Repeat the other instructions.

FORWARD MOVE

This is the most natural move.
We will take an interest in this exercise only as an introduction.
The more complex forms of the exercise can be found:
- either in other situations of movements
- or in several other themes.

INTRODUCTION

Objectives   A normal run in order to intercede in all situations

Organization   Mark the boundary of the run with posts and exercise within the goal.

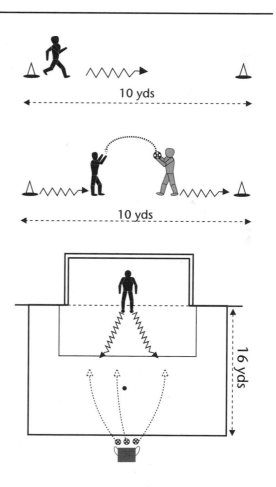

1st situation   Normal run; insist on the limited range of the strides.
a) arms free.
b) Ball held with both hands.
c) Two players: a ball is thrown by a server who steps back as the goalkeeper steps forward.

2nd situation   The goalkeeper stands in his goal area. The ball is hand-thrown then kicked by a server between the 6 yd line and the penalty area (server at 18 yd line). The goalkeeper moves and masters the ball as quickly as possible.
Vary the trajectories of the ball (high, low, medium) and directions (right-left-straight).

EMPHASIS (points to success)

✳ ✳ ✳   When closer to the ball, shorten the stride progressively, (get ready for the take off).

BACKWARD MOVEMENTS
fencing steps

INTRODUCTION

Objectives — Well balanced move (no backward cross-steps) following a lobbed ball along the line (just behind the goalkeeper) for a catch or a dive.

Organization — Between two posts, then in front of the goal, move using backward fencing steps.

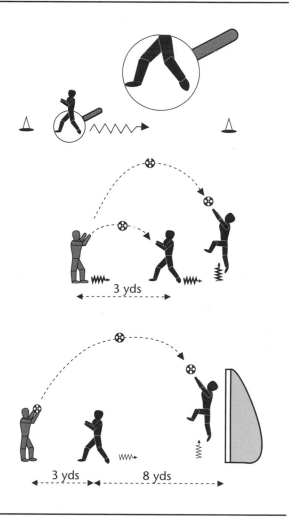

1st situation — In slow motion, without a ball, arms free then bent, hands shoulder-level.
A: one length right foot backward.
B: one length left foot backward.
C: alternate every three strides.

2nd situation — Identical to the first but with a ball held with both hands, arms bent and ball at shoulder-level.

3rd situation — Two players move and exchange balls.
1) At shoulder level
2) High up (this exercise only refers to the goalkeeper who steps back).
(as 1st situation with A: then B: then C:).

N.B. — The ball which is out of line with the main line will determine the choice of the backward step.
• If the ball is on the right hand side of the goalkeeper his right foot will remain behind.
• If the ball is on the left hand side of the goalkeeper, his his left foot will remain behind.

4th situation — Position the exercise in a goal area with a lobbed ball (slow lob), on the main line, above the goalkeeper's head.
(as 1st situation with A: then B: then C:).

EMPHASIS (points to success)

✳ ✳ ✳ Position the backward foot perpendicular to the forward foot (see magnifying glass above)
✳ ✳ ✳ Weight should be on the soles of the feet, heels off the ground.
✳ Strides must be short and low.
✳ ✳ Block the pelvis (contract the abdominal muscles) with shoulders facing the game.
✳ Keep the eyes on the ball.
✳ Arms half bent in a waiting position.
✳ Balance the body at the moment of the impetus.
✳ ✳ ✳ When catching or diving for the ball, take off and landing must be on the backward leg.

II IMPROVEMENT

Objective   The moves must be fast without any loss of balance backwards.
A combination of moves (back and forth).

Organization Exercises in front of the goal.

1st situation   1) The server shoots through a mini goal formed by 2 cones 2 yds apart; his kick is moderate.
2) As soon as the ball is kicked, the goalkeeper, who is positioned in the 6 yd area, catches the ball. (catch or dive).
3) The server then hand throws a lobbed ball in the 6 yd area.
4) The goalkeeper moves with fencing-steps in order to intercept the ball.

2nd situation   Identical to the first, but with a striker who tries to retrieve the ball on a lobbed throw (moderate opposition).

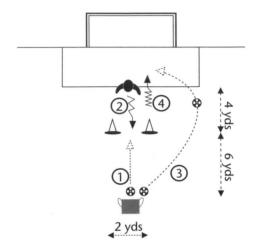

For both situations, vary the position of the mini-goal (facing the goal or on the sides).

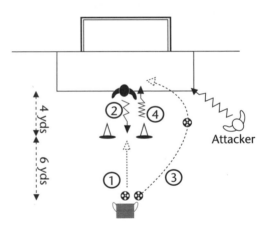

EMPHASIS (points to success)

✳✳   Remain balanced on the ground and in the air.
✳   Increase the speed of movement, restrict the use of the dive.
✳   Remain clear-sighted when and if in contact with the opponent.

III TRAINING

Objective Adapt the movement to the trajectory of the ball and to the opponents (duel). Same intensity as in a real game.

Organization Exercise to be carried out in the penalty area near the goal or in the goal.

1st situation Three servers at 18 yds from the goal area. One goalkeeper and a striker, side by side at 9 yds from the goal area. As soon as the ball is thrown, duel one to one to catch the ball.
• the player tries to score.
• the goalkeeper tries to save the ball

N.B. The server tries a throw in the air and attacks any rebound in the 6 yd area. Vary the servers of the ball.

2nd situation Three servers, each facing a mini-goal and two strikers in the 6 yd area.
Once the starter (1) is under way towards one of the three mini-goals, the corresponding server tries to score (2).
As soon as he has scored or if the ball is intercepted by a dive from the goalkeeper, he hand throws (lobs) another ball (3) towards one of the two strikers so that the latter may head the ball.
The goalkeeper steps back (4) to catch the ball (striker against goalkeeper). Balls are thrown then kicked.

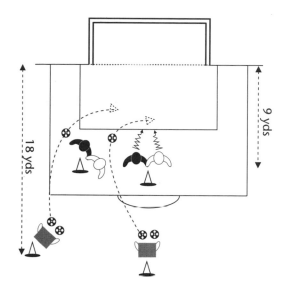

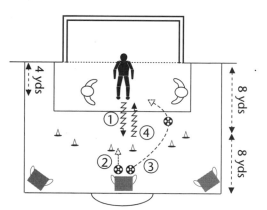

EMPHASIS (points to success)

✱ ✱ The kicking of the ball must be adapted to the level of coaching of the goalkeeper (power and speed).

✱ ✱ Remain balanced in all circumstances (in the movement and contact with the opponent).

✱ ✱ Unfailing mind – guts - willpower (never admit defeat).

BACKWARD: LATERAL MOVEMENTS
cross-steps

I INTRODUCTION

Objectives   Well balanced diagonal backward step (left and right) to catch a ball or dive.

Organization   Three cones in a triangle. Begin at the top cone then backward step towards each of the other cones (right and left).

1st situation   Slow cross-step movement without a ball. (Exercises to be carried out right and then left).

2nd situation   Identical to the first but the ball is held with both hands, arms bent, ball at shoulder level.

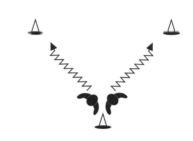

3rd situation   The goalkeeper catches a slow lobbed ball, thrown by a server towards one of the cones.
A: Right (anticipate foot movement).
B: Left (anticipate foot movement).
C: Both feet on the same line in order to be able to move either right or left.

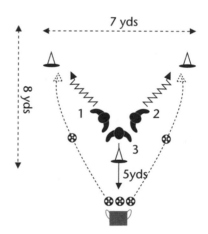

Important   The movement begins with one leg held back then a cross-step (legs uncrossed to begin with).

N.B.   Avoid anticipation.
Begin the exercise only when the ball has been thrown.

EMPHASIS (points to success)

- ✳ ✳ Cross the legs (the moving leg must cross in front of the other one).
- ✳ ✳ Shoulders towards the game (perpendicular to the legs).
- ✳ Eyes always on the ball.
- ✳ Arms bent.
- ✳ ✳ Short strides to avoid a rotation of the pelvis.
- ✳ ✳ ✳ On the jump, uncross legs.
- ✳ ✳ ✳ Take off and landing on backward leg.
- ✳ Remain balanced during the whole movement.

II IMPROVEMENT

Objective   Quick transfer of movements for different situations.

Organization Exercises within and in front of the goal area.

1st situation   Intervention on a crossed ball.
The goalkeeper at the near post.
The server at 5 yds, on the goal line, passes
the ball to a player at 6 to 9 yds and at the
level of the far post. The goalkeeper tries to
intercept the crosses:
A: right
B: left
Throw or kick the ball on the ground then
into the air.

Important   **Try to intercept the ball.**

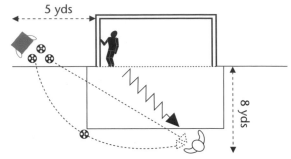

2nd situation   The goalkeeper is at the penalty spot.
A striker at 18 yds dribbles forward and at 16
yds tries to pass to the right or to the left of
the goalkeeper. He has two possibilities:
1-long ground pass
Intervention of the goalkeeper on a low ball
2-Catch the ball and hand lob
Intervention of the goalkeeper on a high ball
A: right side only
B: left side only
C: Alternate left and right

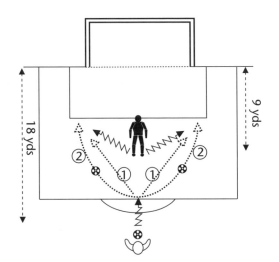

EMPHASIS (points to success)

Reminder of the basic exercises (see introduction)
* ✳ Progressive increase of the speed on a technically adapted move; limit the dive.
* ✳ ✳ Adapt quickly to each situation (reflex).
* ✳ ✳ Co-ordinate the move followed by a throw or a dive.

III TRAINING

Objective   Look for movements combined with the catch of the ball, high throws or dives with real opponents (one against one, goalkeeper against goalkeeper or inclusion of field players).

Organization Two goals set close together.

1st situation   Two goalkeepers at their near posts.
At 20 yds, the server throws or kicks (ground, lob or half-lob) the balls, seeking an equidistant throw to the two goals and at the level of the far posts. As soon as the balls are thrown, cross steps then duel one against one to catch the ball.
The goalkeepers change goals after each throw.

2nd situation   Identical to the first, but with one or more field players (partners and opponents) replacing the second goalkeeper.
A more or less dynamic opposition depending on the level of the goalkeeper.

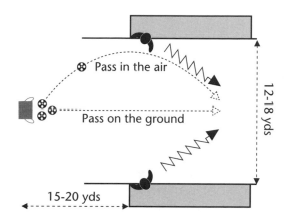

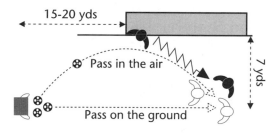

EMPHASIS (points to success)

✹ ✹   An appropriate position at the beginning of each situation (feet and torso facing the game).

   ✹   Adapt the speed of movement to the trajectory of the ball.

✹ ✹   Maintain a body balance when moving despite contact with the opponent.

✹ ✹   Guts – willpower during the duel are a requirement.

CROSSED STEPS PRECEDING THE DIVE TO THE GROUND

This chapter should only be tackled when the goalkeeper has learned lateral diving.

I INTRODUCTION

Objectives   Speedy intervention on a straight ball at post level.

Organization   Mark a goal with two cones. Choose soft ground (grass).

1st situation	The ball is at 3 yards and on the same line as the goalkeeper. Cross the legs then push with the outside leg to catch the ball. Exercise to be carried out in slow motion (breakdown of the movement). Work to the right and left.
2nd situation	Identical to the first, with ball held with both hands.
3rd situation	Identical to the first, but a server, at 5 yds from the goalkeeper, throws the ball at ground level, right then left.
4th situation	Identical to the third, but in a goal area with a throw then a kick at the base of the opposite post.

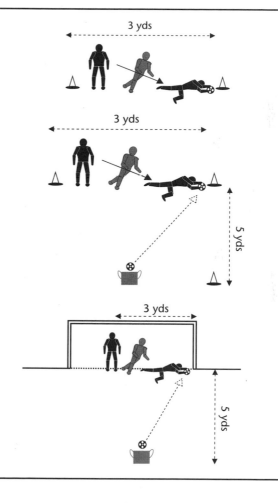

EMPHASIS (points to success)

✱   Eyes on the ball.

✱ ✱ ✱   Shift weight towards the ball (pelvis initiates movement).

✱ ✱ ✱   Cross legs forward.

✱ ✱ ✱   Uncross legs when diving and initiate push with the outside leg (free the knee and the foot of the outside leg).

Important: **Outside leg = leg furthest from** the ball
                  Inside leg = leg nearest to the ball

II IMPROVEMENT

Objective   A combination of two interventions (to the left and to the right).

Organization Exercises to be carried out in the goal area.

1st situation   The goalkeeper begins in the middle of the goal area.
The server is at 5 yds
The goalkeeper dives on all the balls which are thrown in his direction at approx. 2.5 yds alternating right then left (straight kick at ground level).
After the first ball, the goalkeeper gets up as fast as possible for the second ball.

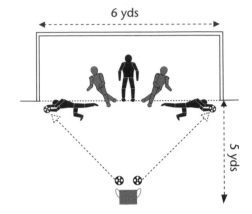

2nd situation   Identical to the first but a striker screens the goalkeeper and intercepts all dropped balls.

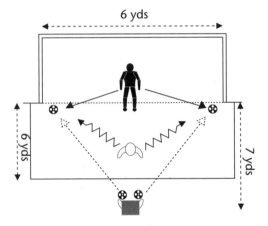

EMPHASIS (points to success)

* ✳   Increase speed of the exercise.
* ✳ ✳   Master right and left moves.
* ✳ ✳   Co-ordinate adapted body movements (combine the dive to the movement).

III TRAINING

Objective   Apply a maximum of speed despite a dynamic opposition.
Apply all the techniques of body movement as in a real game.

Organization Use of the goal area, the 6 yd area and the penalty area.

1st situation   **Organization:**
• A goal at 4 yds divided into two equal sections.
• A screen player in the 6 yd area
• A striker at 7 yds from the goal.
The opponent tries to score.
Area including a goalkeeper = free kick = 1 point
Area without a goalkeeper = kick to the ground = 3 points
The moving screen player only conceals the goalkeeper's field of vision.
The goalkeeper intervenes on all the balls.
The exercise is to be carried out with the goalkeeper to the right then to the left of the goal area.

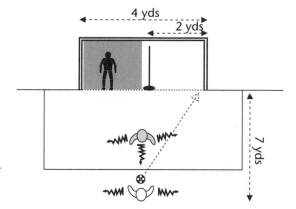

2nd situation   **Organization:**
• two mini-goals (width: 1 yd; height: 0.50 yds) in a 6 yd wide goal area.
• The goalkeeper remains in the center of the goal (mini-goal area forbidden).
• Four players in the penalty area but outside the 6 yd area.
Match two against two: try to score in one of the two mini-goals without going beyond the 6 yd area.
The goalkeeper may only intercede within the mini-goals, using his arms.

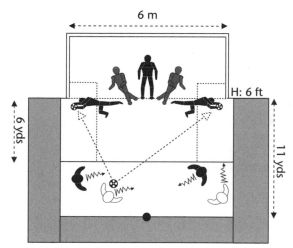

EMPHASIS (points to success)

✳✳✳   React quickly on all shots (intensity of the match).
✳   Stand in the right area despite the opposition (the ball must be in view).
✳✳   Try to block or veer the ball to the side (corner).

GAMES

I INTRODUCTION ————————————————

"10 PASSES"

Objectives   Use the appropriate moves according to each situation despite opposition.

Organization   In a square, 7 yds x 7 yds, two against two, three against three or four against four, depending on the number of goalkeepers.

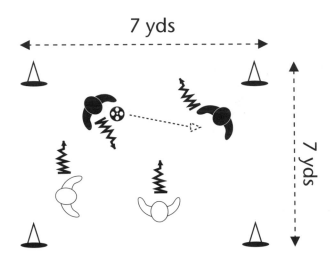

ACTION
Each team tries to pass the ball 10 times while running, without the opposite team intercepting it.

Three options for throwing: free pass
                                       ground pass   (vary the options)
                                       high pass

1: As soon as the 10 passes have been carried out, the team gets 1 point and hands the ball over to the other team.
2: If the ball is caught before the 10 passes have been carried out, the exercise begins again and the game continues.
3: Try to include all different kinds of moves adapted to the trajectory of the ball and the movements of teammates and opponents.

Count the number of points won by each team in a given time.

II IMPROVEMENT

THE COLLECTOR

Objectives   A combination of all kinds of moves (forward-back-lateral-side and fencing steps).
Adapt to the various trajectories of the ball and to powerful kicks.
Moderate opposition.

Organization
- one goalkeeper
- one or several strikers
- three servers (two at 15 yds on the wings, one at 10 yds on the main line) distribute the balls alternately.

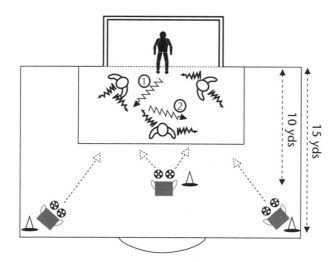

ACTION
- The goalkeeper must fetch as many balls thrown in the 6 yd area as possible.
- The strikers only move in the 6 yd area.

Two possibilities:
1 • They try to catch the ball and throw it to the servers.
2 • They try to catch the ball and score.

- One of the three servers throws another ball as soon as the previous one has been caught (do not give the goalkeeper time to stand on his line).
- Rest after every 10 balls.
- At the end of each exercise, count the number of balls saved by the goalkeeper.

III TRAINING

THE RUNNER

Objectives   The goalkeeper uses all kinds of moves depending on the game. He must therefore adapt to:
- the trajectory of the ball
- the strength of the kick
- how the opponents are placed

Insist on the appropriate technique for each situation and correct if necessary.

Organization The field is demarcated by the 6 yd area (plus extension) and the penalty area

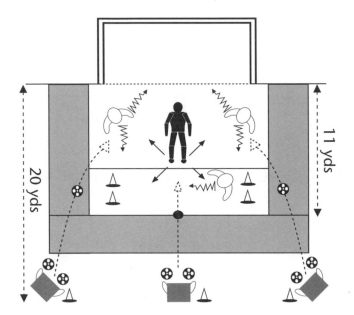

ACTION
- The servers hand out, either:

1: to the players in the 6 yd area (high pass) so that they may score in the main goal. Value: 3 points to a goal.

Or: 2: to the players outside the 6 yd area (free pass) so that they may score in one of the two mini-goals. Value: 1 point.

The choice of the server will depend on where the goalkeeper is positioned.

N.B. a new ball is thrown as soon as: a goal is scored,
the ball is caught by the goalkeeper,
the ball goes out of bounds.

Physical recovery of the goalkeeper after each set of 5 to 8 balls.
- At the end of each set, count the number of balls caught by the goalkeeper.

SPECIFIC SPEED

As **it develops**, modern soccer tends to give priority to speed.

The goalkeeper is no exception to the rule. As there **is less space in the penalty area** for the strikers, the same applies to the goalkeeper.

Dummy passes and **lifted trajectories** increase the possibilities of **tricks**.

Consequently, **the goalkeeper must see and act with speed.**
Everything happens in **seconds**. He must therefore take a **maximum of adapted and sound decisions** in a **minimum amount of time**.

Nevertheless, there exist different speeds. **The coach should train the future goal-keepers separately then together, and plan their physical recovery period very carefully.**

We will therefore study:

- Body speed   35
- Speed of reaction   39
- Ground speed   43
- Reflex speed   47
- Games   50

BODY SPEED

I INTRODUCTION

Objectives   Standing still and without opposition, handle the ball in order to increase the rhythm of the catch, retaining the correct body movement.

Organization   One ball for each of the goalkeepers.

1st situation	In a standing position, rotate the ball around the waist, right and left (no contact with the body).

2nd situation	Legs apart, the ball is held between the legs (one hand forward, one hand backward). Change hands without the ball touching the ground.

3rd situation	Legs apart, the ball is held behind the body. Let go of the ball then half rotate the body to catch it on the other side before it touches the ground (throw the ball nearer and nearer the ground).

4th situation	In a standing position, the ball is held with one hand behind the body. Let go of the ball then half rotate the body to catch the ball on the other side before it touches the ground (throw the ball nearer and nearer the ground).

5th situation	The ball is held between the legs. Throw it vertically into the air from between the legs, then catch it as quickly as possible.

EMPHASIS (points to success)

* ✹ ✹   Concentrate on the quality of the catch in all situations.
* ✹   Master the body balance.
* ✹   Ease of the movements.
  Try to increase the speed of the exercise.

II IMPROVEMENT

Objectives A combination of situations with two or more players, with various trajectories of the ball and adapting quickly to the new situation.

Organization With two or more players, one ball each.

1st situation At a standstill, simultaneous exchange of balls with two goalkeepers(one ball each).
A: Direct throws
B: Rebounding throws
C: One direct throw, the other by rebound.
The exercise begins with one of the goalkeepers throwing his ball (starter).

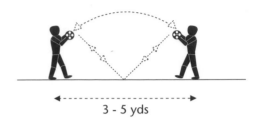

3 - 5 yds

2nd situation At a standstill and with two players.
One goalkeeper throws the ball vertically (1) (above his head), blocks the ball thrown by the partner (2), throws it back at him (3), and catches his ball before it hits the ground (4).

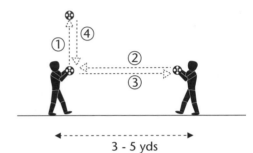

3 - 5 yds

3rd situation Three players are positioned in a triangle. One goalkeeper throws his ball vertically (above his head), and tries to catch his partner's ball before it touches the ground. The starter is one of the goalkeepers who begins the exercise by throwing his ball. Determine the rotation.
To be carried out to the right then to the left.

3 - 5 yds

EMPHASIS (points to success)

✳ ✳   Always master the ball.
✳   Permanent concentration.
     Increase the speed of the exercise.

III TRAINING

Objectives   Mastery of the body movement in all situations despite a dynamic opposition (tackle) as in a real game situation.

Organization   Use a reduced size goal area.

1st situation   Within a 4 yd goal area, the goalkeeper must catch all the balls thrown by a server standing 6 to 8 yds from the goal, despite two or three strikers in charge of screening him and scoring on any rebounds. Play first with thrown balls, then with kicks.

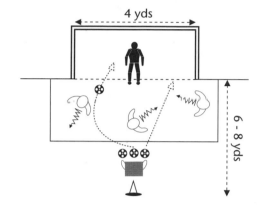

2nd situation   In a 4 yd goal area, two goalkeepers, one against the other.
Identical to the 1st, but:
    a) without strikers
    b) with strikers
The server tries to score.

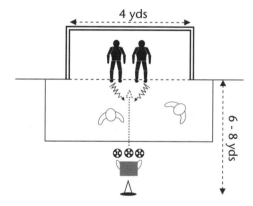

EMPHASIS (points to success)

✳ ✳ ✳ Avoid letting go of the balls in any circumstances (quality of the moves)
  ✳ ✳ Remain balanced despite the opposition.
  ✳ ✳ Avoid anticipating.
    ✳ Willpower – guts.

SPEED OF REACTION

I INTRODUCTION

Objectives   A response to a visual, sensorial or auditive signal.
Progressively reduce the existing time lapse between the information and the reaction (latent period).

Organization Two players with one or three balls (3rd exercise).

1st situation   The goalkeeper is facing away from the server (at 3 yds).
The ball is thrown towards his back.
As soon as there is contact, half rotation of the goalkeeper to catch the ball before it touches the ground.

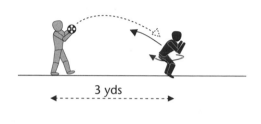

2nd situation The goalkeeper is facing away from the server (at 3 yds).
The ball is thrown either to the ground (between the legs to the right then to the left), or in the air near the goalkeeper.
As soon as the latter sees the ball, he must try to catch it as quickly as possible (frequent use of the dive).

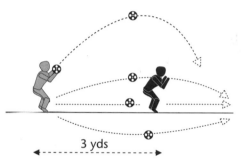

3rd situation The coach points to one of the three balls set down on the ground in front of the goalkeeper.
At a signal, the goalkeeper must, with a dive, grab the chosen ball as quickly as possible.

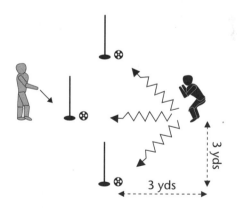

EMPHASIS (points to success)

✳ ✳ ✳ Begin with an adequate basic position, i.e. legs flexed, heels off the ground, flat back, eyes forward, arms flexed, hands positioned to catch the ball.

✳ ✳ Avoid anticipating.

✳ ✳ Heavy concentration.

II IMPROVEMENT

Objectives   A combination of various situations.
  • Speed reaction followed by a catch or a dive.

Organization   Exercises to be carried out in front of a wall for the 2nd and 3rd situations.

1st situation   Three goalkeepers, lateral side-stepping. The goalkeeper in the center moves and catches the first ball, throws it back to the server, then half rotates to face the other server and carries on by catching another ball.

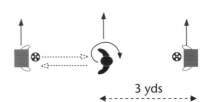

2nd situation   Two players: the goalkeeper facing the wall, a server behind him.
The latter throws the ball against the wall (by hand then kick).
The goalkeeper reacts straight away after the rebound to avoid the goal.
The server can move.

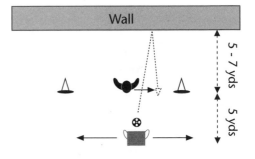

3rd situation   Identical to the 2nd, only the goalkeeper faces the server.
  • As soon as the ball is thrown, half rotation of the goalkeeper followed by the appropriate reaction.

Variation   If no wall is available, it is possible to use a player who hand-shoots back or kicks.

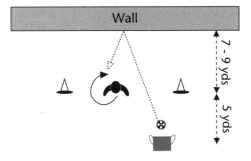

EMPHASIS (points to success)

✻ ✻ ✻   Implement the half turns to the right and to the left with the same ease.
  ✻ ✻   Maintain body balance after the half turn in order to master the ball.
    ✻   Increase the speed.
  ✻ ✻   Heavy concentration during the exercise.
    ✻   Check the quality of the catch.

III TRAINING

Objectives   Set up game situations without, then with a more or less dynamic opposition(s) (starter=ball).

Organization Exercises carried out in the penalty area with use of the goal.

1st situation   The goalkeeper is in the goal facing the game.
The server stands behind the goal. He throws the ball (which is invisible to the goalkeeper) to one of the three strikers who stand outside the 6 yd area.
The latter tries to score on the volley (head or foot).
As soon as the ball is kicked, the goalkeeper intervenes.

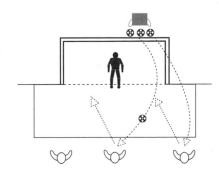

2nd situation   Identical to the first, but a striker disturbs the goalkeeper in the 6 yd area and tries to score if there is a rebound.

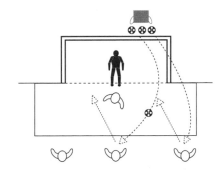

3rd situation   The goalkeeper is in the goal.
The strikers drive their ball in a limited area (between the penalty spot and the 18 yd line).
When one of the strikers steps in the zone, near the goal area, the goalkeeper intercedes. (the striker can only score within the 6 yd area).
a) Without a screen-player in the 6 yd area.
b) With a screen player in the 6 yd area.

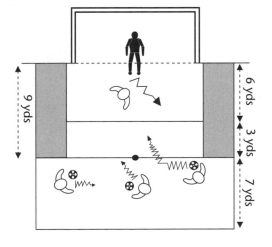

EMPHASIS (points to success)

✳ ✳ ✳   Reduce the rest period to a strict minimum.
  ✳ ✳   Remain permanently balanced in all situations.
  ✳ ✳   Constant concentration.
    ✳   Courage – willpower.

GROUND SPEED

I INTRODUCTION

Objective   Try to go from the standing position to the sitting position as quickly as possible.

Organization Use either the ball or the server as a starter.

1st situation   The server moves with the ball.
As soon as he sets the ball on the ground, the goalkeeper must lie down in order to catch it as quickly as possible (2).

2nd situation   The goalkeeper is lying on his side, arms extended.
As soon as a ball is thrown at his feet, he must stand up to catch it as quickly as possible.

3rd situation   The server, starter of the exercise, holds a ball in each hand, arms in a horizontal position.
The goalkeeper, at 1 yd from the server, is in a waiting position.
As soon as the server lets go of one of the balls, the goalkeeper must catch it before it bounces (he must lie down).

EMPHASIS (points to success)

✳ ✳ ✳   Remain in basic adequate position (waiting): (see 3rd situation above)
heels off the ground.
  • legs bent.
  • straight back.
  • arms flexed, hands raised.
  • eyes staring straight ahead.
✳ ✳   Intervention as soon as the signal is given (the ball is either lying on the ground or released).
✳ ✳   Avoid anticipating.
✳ ✳   Heavy concentration.

II IMPROVEMENT

Objectives   A combination of situations (i.e.: stretching to catch the ball followed by ground - swiftness exercises) without, then with a moderate opposition.

Organization   Two, then one ball only. Set up a mini-goal.

1st situation   The server throws a ball up, the goalkeeper stretches to catch it (1) and throws it back, then lies down on a ball which is on the ground (2).

2nd situation   Identical to the 1st, only the goalkeeper himself throws the ball up (1), then lies down on the one on the ground (2) and stands up to catch his first ball before it touches the ground (3).

3rd situation   The goalkeeper throws the ball at a striker's chest (standing sideways) who chests it towards the ground.
The goalkeeper follows his ball and catches it before it touches the ground.
Exercise to be carried out right then left.

4th situation   Identical to the 3rd situation, only the striker is in control facing a mini-goal and settles the ball in order to shoot and score. The goalkeeper leaves his area after the ball has been thrown and intercedes before the shot (dive to the feet).

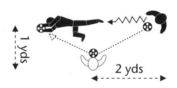

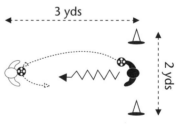

EMPHASIS (points to success)

✳ ✳ ✳   Maintain speed when implementing the exercise.
   ✳   Remain concentrated.
   ✳ ✳   Courage – willpower.

III TRAINING

Objectives Ground speed in various game situations, with more or less dynamic opposition.

Organization Use the penalty area and a goal.

1st situation High center or ground pass with guided control by the striker towards the 6 yd area and near the goal. Intervention of the goalkeeper after mastering the ball.
• the striker is at a standstill, then moves.
• several strikers and defenders can be included.
Work to the right and the left.

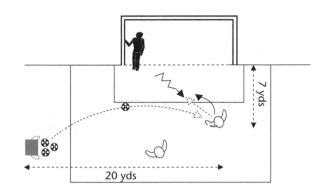

2nd situation Identical to the 1st, only the ball is kicked head-on (the striker turns his back to the goalkeeper on the 6 yd line).
The server passes to the striker who then opts:
• either for a channeled control before the shot
• or sell a body dummy to surprise the goalkeeper.
The goalkeeper intervenes in both cases.
Several strikers and defenders can be included.

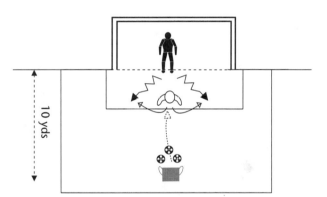

EMPHASIS (points to success)

✳ ✳   Adapt very quickly to the situation.
✳ ✳   Avoid premature anticipation.
   ✳   Plan the choice well (what to do and when?).
   ✳   Insist on the quality of the command (clear order for the partners).
   ✳   Courage – Willpower in all circumstances.

REFLEX SPEED

I INTRODUCTION

The exercises in this section should only be undertaken
after the goalkeeper has adequately mastered the following themes:

- **THE PHYSICAL PREPARATION and particularly:**
    - Movements (sidesteps – crossed steps – forward run)
    - Specific speed (body movement – reaction- ground speed)
    - Co-ordination

- **THE TECHNICAL PREPARATION and particularly:**
    - catching the ball
    - the dives (lateral and forward)

The young goalkeeper will then be able to acquire a physical maturity and a well
established command of the body, both of which are indispensable in addressing
this subject

IN COMPLETE SAFETY.

* * *

II IMPROVEMENT

Objectives A combination of situations without opponents, and intervention on a straight and close shot.

Organization Use of a goal area (2 by 3 yds) and a low, then a high fence.

1st situation A goalkeeper in a goal area, 3 yds wide.
A straight shot by the striker at goal (facing or sideways).
He follows his shot in order to score on any rebound.

2nd situation Two footed jump by the goalkeeper over a low fence, landing in a mini goal (2 yds). As soon as he has landed, the striker kicks the ball (straight kick).

3rd situation Identical to the second, only the goalkeeper goes under a high fence.

Important Adapt the height of the fence to the goalkeeper in the 2nd and 3rd situations.
• low fence = between 20 and 50 inches
• high fence = between 100 and 150 inches

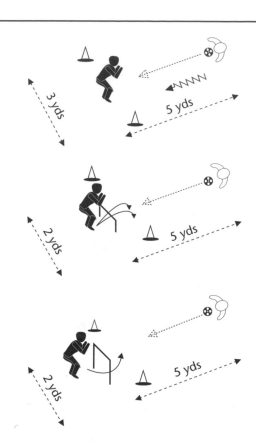

EMPHASIS (points to success)

✳ ✳ Always return to the basic position before the next save: legs flexed, heels off the ground, eyes on the ball, arms bent, straight torso.

✳ ✳ Seek a quick positioning of the body on the trajectory of the ball (efficiency).

✳ Remain in a positive and dynamic attitude (avoid apprehension).

✳ Great concentration should be maintained.

✳ Courage – willpower.

III TRAINING

Objectives Incorporate the exercises in a game situation i.e. with real speed and a dynamic opposition.

Organization Exercises to be carried out in the goal.

1st situation The goalkeeper is in his area at the near post (closing the angle).
Cross from a striker who stands on the goal line to a partner at 8 yds from the goal.
As soon as the pass has been made, the goalkeeper positions himself again and intercedes on the kick.
Exercises to be carried out right and left.

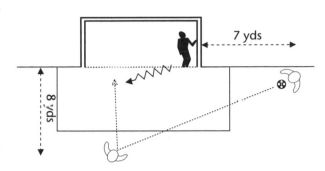

2nd situation The goalkeeper stands in his goal and pays attention to a high cross (in the 6 yd area). He intercedes on the cross by catching or deflecting the ball and positions himself straight away to intercede on a second ball kicked by another striker at 7 yds from the goal.
Exercise to be carried out right and left.
It is possible to incorporate one or more attackers in the 6 yd area, then one or more opponents.

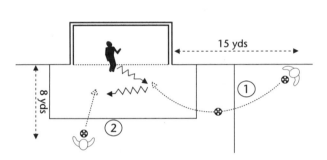

EMPHASIS (points to success)

✳ ✳ ✳ Quality of the moves, movements and repositioning.
✳ ✳ ✳ Maintain well balanced supports (stabilize on the soles of the feet, heels off the ground).
  ✳ ✳ The sequence of movements is to be carried out quickly.
    ✳ Courage – willpower
    ✳ Look for maximum power in the kicks.

THE GAMES

I INTRODUCTION

THE KNOCK OUT

Objectives   Use the various appropriate speeds with a view of efficiency despite the presence of a striker.

Organization Four goals (width: 4 yds) and four goalkeepers in a field,15 yds x 15 yds. A striker is in charge of catching the ball released by the goalkeepers.

Development The goalkeeper who has the ball tries to score in one of the 3 other goals by clearing the ball by hand (a direct throw or bounce).
Any ball which has not been mastered by the goalkeeper is played by the striker.
The goalkeeper who scores exchanges with the striker (if the latter is a goalkeeper).

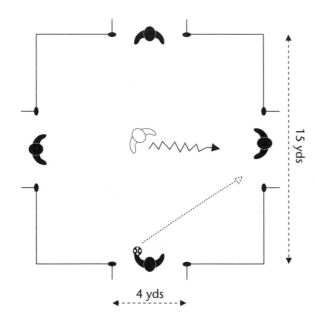

15 yds

4 yds

N.B. The field size and the width of the goals can vary depending on the categories and the level of success in the interventions.

If the striker is not a goalkeeper, count the number of scores in a given time (10 to 15 minutes).

II IMPROVEMENT

HODGE-PODGE

Objectives   A combination of situations (various moves + speeds) at a faster rhythm with pressing opponents.

Organization • a field 10 x 10 yds with goals 4 yds wide.
    • 2 or 3 goal areas with two sides and one goalkeeper for each area.
    • a team of 2 or 3 strikers.

Development For three minutes, the strikers try to score in both sides of all the goals.

After the three minutes, exchange teams.

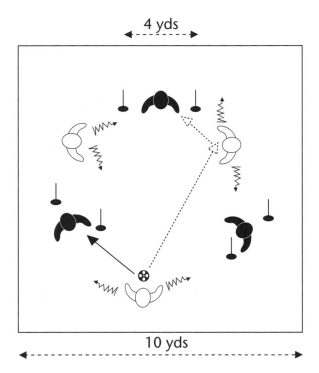

Count the number of goals scored after each switch.

III TRAINING

THE FLIPPER

Objectives   Highlight the quality of speed of the goalkeepers through high intensity exercises (favor reflex-speed). In addition to speed, clear headedness, courage, guts and willpower are emphasized.

Organization   • A field 12 x 12 yds.
   • Two goals 4 yds wide.
   • Three groups of players   1st group = two goalkeepers
                                   2nd group = two strikers
                                   3rd group = two servers

Development   After a server has passed the ball (servers take turns) the strikers try to score with the first touch in one of the two goals (possibility of passes between them).
   The goalkeepers intervene as soon as the ball is in play.
   After intervention by the goalkeeper, the exit of the ball or a goal, a new ball is handed out.
   Rotate the teams after sending ten balls (five from each server).

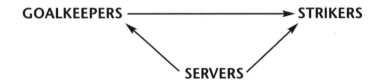

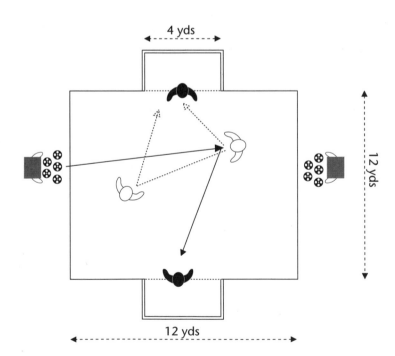

N.B.   The size of the field can be changed depending on the categories and level of success in the interventions.

Count the number of goals scored after each series of 10 balls.

COORDINATION - SUPPORT

These days, in every match, the **relative density of the defense does not** allow the goalkeeper to take a straight and regular **approach**.

He is going to have to **dodge, modify his ground support, link movements** and maintain a **perfect balance** in all situations.

It is up to him to **choose what is technically the best move** and to **use a one or two foot take off** or **stand his ground** in order to **intercede** in the best conditions.

We will therefore study:

THE APPROACH

I INTRODUCTION

Objective   Move forward, backward or diagonally.
Priority is given to quality, breaking down the movement, then including simple combinations (run up followed by a right foot take off, a left foot take off or a take off with both feet).

Organization   Implementation of the exercise in a defined area.

1st situation   Refer to the topic on simple moves, such as: lateral, backward-side moves, backward, forward moves.

2nd situation   The mirror game.
The goalkeeper moves following the visual order of the coach (gesture of the arm) either towards him, away from him, to the right or to the left.

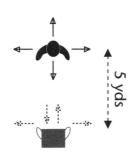

3rd situation   Forward movement with a right foot take off, left foot take off, or two footed take off, (following the gesture of the coach) at a line drawn on the ground.
Exercises to be carried out first without, then with a ball.

EMPHASIS (points to success)

✳ ✳   Limit the range of the strides (short strides to prepare for a take-off).
✳   Use any form of movement to remain facing the starter.
✳   Retain body balance in all circumstances (heels off the ground, legs bent, eyes fixed on the starter or the ball, arms bent).

II IMPROVEMENT

Objective   Incorporate approaches with various combinations
Introduction of obstacles or players.

Organization Use cones and hurdles to form a course.

1st situation   Run from one cone to another, crossing
an area obstructed by a number of obstacles
(cones, posts, free areas, fences).
Possibility of using various moves
(forward, backward, lateral).

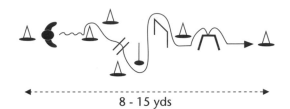

8 - 15 yds

2nd situation Identical to the first, but the obstacles are
replaced by players.
(Moderate then dynamic opposition).

3rd situation   Identical to the second; include a throw
of a high ball after the slalom.

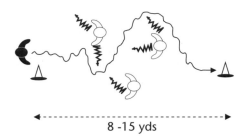

8 -15 yds

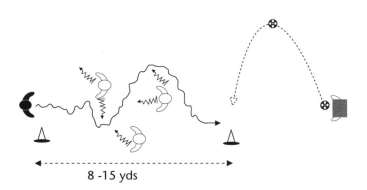

8 -15 yds

EMPHASIS (points to success)

  ✸ ✸   Retain body balance despite the obstacles.
  ✸ ✸   Maintain pace (do not slow down).
    ✸   Stress the peripheral vision (you must see the obstacles, the opponents and the ball).
    ✸   Keep the body facing the "finish" mark.

III TRAINING

Objective In a game situation and with dynamic opposition, movements will be followed by impulse combined with certain types of technical moves (catch, dive etc.).

Organization Use of a goal area and the 6 yd area.
Servers are on the 18 yd line.

1st situation The goalkeeper intercedes on all the balls kicked in the 6 yd area despite opponents in his way.

2nd situation Post strikers who will try to score and defenders who will try to clear the ball. The field players are positioned between the goal line and the 9 yd area.

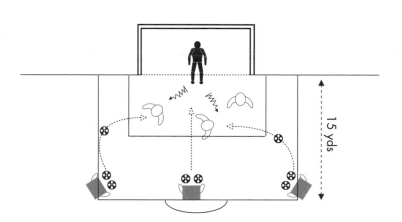

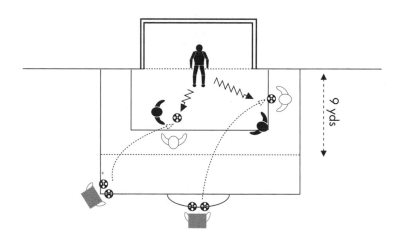

EMPHASIS (points to success)

✳ ✳   Choose an adapted run-up (remain well balanced when catching the ball).
✳ ✳   The order must be loud and clear to warn the opponents.
✳   Show decisiveness.
✳   Courage – willpower
✳   Watch the competence of the goalkeeper in stepping without shuffling.

TWO-FOOT TAKE OFF

I INTRODUCTION

Objective   A varied impulse will co-ordinate ground supports.

Organization   Use the lines marking the boundary of the field then use hoops and cones.

1st situation	Skipping on the spot. Two foot take off landing on one or both feet.
2nd situation	Identical to the first with a skipping rope.
3rd situation	While moving, make progress by jumping laterally over a line.
4th situation	Identical to the third; jump over lined up cones.
5th situation	Hoops have been lined up. Two forward jumps against one backward jump in the hoops.
N.B.	The exercises are to be carried out without, then with a ball in hand (apart from the rope). A server may throw the ball during or at the end of the situation.

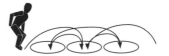

EMPHASIS (points to success)

✳ ✳ ✳ Feet are to be placed at the same level (heels off the ground).

✳ ✳ Keep the body balanced during the take off and the landing.

✳ ✳ Eyes are horizontal (look straight ahead).

✳ Co-ordinate the move "arm-impulse" (take a run-up with the arms before the leg impulse).

II IMPROVEMENT

Objective   Combine a two-foot take off with a run-up.

Organization Exercises to be carried out in the 6 yd area.

1st situation   The goalkeeper leaves his goal area to intercept all high balls (run-up followed by a two-foot). The second ball is thrown as soon as the first one has been caught.
a) without opponent.
b) with opponent (s) in the 6 yd area.

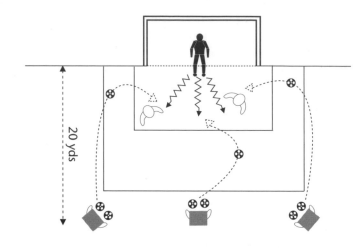

2nd situation   Identical to the first, but linking the catch with a throw towards the servers (opponents at a stand still).
The second ball is thrown immediately after the first one.

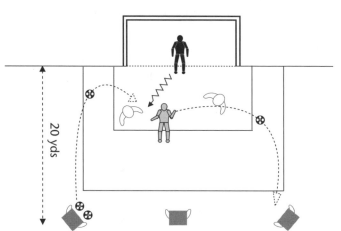

EMPHASIS (points to success)

  ✳ ✳   Combine the run-up with the take off (assess the trajectory).
  ✳ ✳   Position yourself under the ball when catching it in order to use a two-foot take off.
✳ ✳ ✳   Only use the two-foot take off when not pressured by the opponent (safety margin).
  ✳ ✳   The situations are to be carried out at high speed.

III TRAINING

Objective   A combination of various run-ups (forwards, backwards, lateral) followed by the catch of a high ball after a two-foot take off.

Organization   Exercises to be carried out in the penalty area.
The goalkeeper begins on the 6 yd line.

1st situation   The goalkeeper at the 6 yd line.
He intercedes on all high balls thrown alternately, short and long.
HIgh and slow throws.

2nd situation   Identical to the first; include teammates and opponents who will be in the goalkeeper's way.
The second throw takes place as soon as the first ball has been mastered.
High and slow throws.

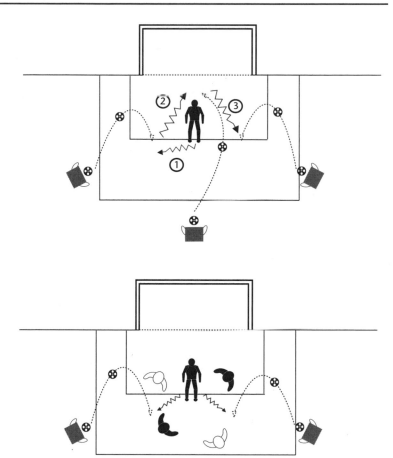

EMPHASIS (points to success)

✹ ✹ ✹   Only carry out a two-foot take off when there is no pressure from the opponent.

✹ ✹ ✹   Position parallel supports in order to avoid an unintentional rotation of the body.

✹ ✹   Retain body balance despite opposition.

✹   Carry out a good co-ordination between the movement and the take off.

✹   Remind players of the different techniques of the moves.

ONE-FOOT TAKE OFF

I INTRODUCTION

Objective   Develop the quality of each jump.

Organization   Use the marking-out of the field and include hoops.

1st situation   Rehearse the 5 situations from "two-foot take off" using a one-foot take off.

2nd situation   Lateral hopping strides in the hoops. The whole weight of the body must be on the supporting leg before changing hoops.
Push off with the outward leg.

3rd situation   Identical to the second with the following variations:

1 • Land on both feet in the hoops then a single foot take off (inward leg then outward leg).
2 • Land on the same foot as the take off leg. New take off on the other foot.
3 • Land on the foot of the free leg and change feet for a new jump.

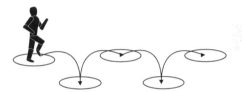

4th situation   Bouncing strides on line, varying the distance between the hoops.

EMPHASIS (points to success)

✳ ✳ Concentrate on the quality of the landing (on the sole of the foot, leg bent).
✳ ✳ Avoid flexing the take off leg too much.

Reminder: Outward leg = the furthest from the next hoop.
Inward leg   = the nearest to the next hoop.

II IMPROVEMENT

Objective A combination of the approach followed by a one-foot take off with various obstacles.

Organization In the goal area using a low hurdle, then bringing in teammates and opponents.

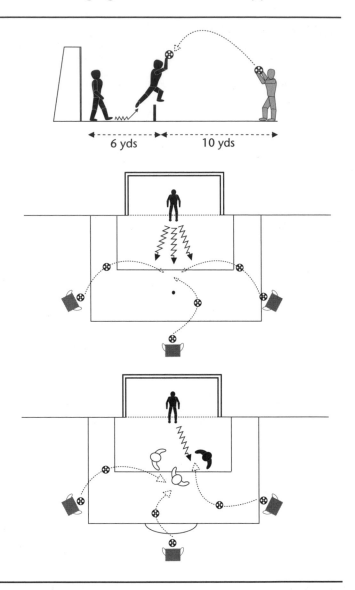

1st situation Begin from the goal area, with a hurdle, 30 inches high on the 6 yd line.
The server throws a high ball to the 6 yd line.
The goalkeeper jumps over the hurdle to catch the ball.
Balanced landing (alternate right-foot take off then left-foot take off).
It is possible to begin the exercise without a hurdle, then vary its height.

2nd situation Servers are positioned straight on line and on the wings and give high throws in the penalty area (between 9 and 6 yds)
The goalkeeper begins on his goal line and with a one-foot take off leaps and stretches to catch the ball.

3rd situation Identical to the second but with a moderate, then a dynamic opposition.
Goalkeeper can catch and distribute to a teammate or clear with a punch.

EMPHASIS (points to success)

❋ ❋ ❋ Choose the take off leg according to the direction of flight. (You must remain facing the game).
  • If the ball comes from the left of the goalkeeper = right leg take off.
  • If the ball comes from the right of the goalkeeper = left leg take off.
❋ ❋ Avoid big strides before the jump.
❋ ❋ ❋ Use the free leg as a supplementary impulse factor, then as a stabilizing element in space (avoid rotating the body) in order to remain facing the game while at the same time protecting yourself from the opponents.
❋ Keep the body well balanced in all situations.

III TRAINING

Objective In a game situation, a combination of various run-ups (forward, backward, lateral) including dynamic opponents and partners.

Organization Exercises to be carried out in the goal (penalty area).

1st situation Intervention by the goalkeeper on high crosses (alternate right and left with duels between the goalkeeper, the strikers and the defenders).
Possibility of a catch of the ball or clearing with the fist.

2nd situation Identical to the first with interventions on high balls thrown on line.

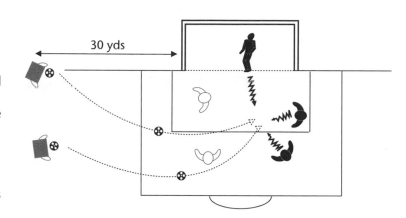

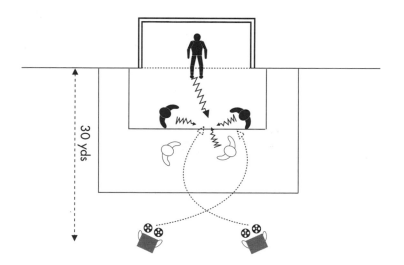

EMPHASIS (points to success)

✳ ✳ Raise the shoulder level at the moment of impact.
✳ Remain balanced in all circumstances.
✳ ✳ A clear order to warn your teammates.
✳ Courage – willpower in the duels.

CHANGING DIRECTION

I INTRODUCTION

Objective　　Concentrate on the quality of the final foot plant before changing direction. Stress the quality of the movements.

Organization　Use hoops and hurdles (or benches).

1st situation　Move forward, setting one foot in each hoop, as quickly as possible. The dragging-step is a must and crossing legs is forbidden.
It is possible to time the course.
It is compulsory to remain facing the game.

2nd situation　Identical to the first, but a second goalkeeper must catch up with the first beginning one hoop behind.

3rd situation　Identical to the first, but a ball is thrown to compel the goalkeeper to look ahead.

4th situation　Jump over a hurdle (height: 20 inches).
Begin facing or sideways. Jump off one or both feet landing on one or both feet with a half or complete turn over the obstacle.
The jumps can be carried out:
　　　• without a ball
　　　• holding a ball
　　　• with a ball thrown by a server.

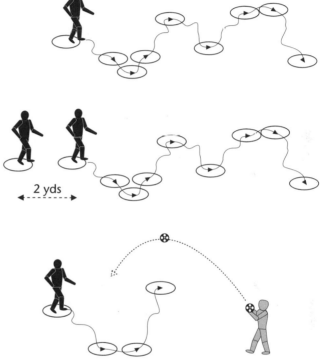

2 yds

EMPHASIS (points to success)

　✳　Quick contact must be made with the outward foot in the hoop (burning hot soil).
✳ ✳　Spread the weight of the body when planting the feet.
✳ ✳　Always look in front of you (do not look at your feet).
　✳　Remain balanced during all moves.

67

II IMPROVEMENT

Objective   Change direction as fast as possible depending on the situations. Include moderate opposition (opponents)

Organization Use hoops, mini-goals and a full-size goal.

1st situation   The goalkeeper must defend two mini-goals situated on his right and on his left while moving forward through several hoops (one step in each hoop). He should move to save any ball thrown towards a mini-goal.

2nd situation   In a mini-goal. High throws alternating right and left. Catch the ball, body extended, then Change direction to catch the second ball in flight.

3rd situation   In a mini-goal. Begin in the center of the goal. With dragging steps, move to touch the post then intervene on the high ball thrown towards one of the three static strikers.

4th situation   Identical to the third, but one of the strikers is moving.

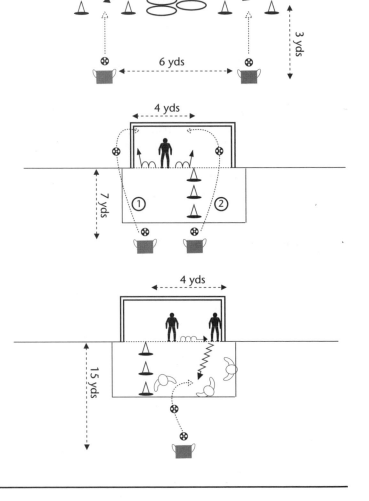

EMPHASIS (points to success)

  ✳ ✳   Remain balanced in order to be able to intercede right and left.
    ✳   Increase the speed of the exercise.
    ✳   Concentrate in order to choose the right move.

III TRAINING

Objective
A combination of direction changes (right, left, in front, behind).
Adapt to the movement of the ball at high speed without, then with opposition.

Organization In front of the goal.
- movement of the goalkeeper in front of an arc situated in the 6 yd area.
- movement of the strikers in front of an arc situated in the 18 yd area.

1st situation
Intervention of the goal - keeper on all the straight or lobbed shots, preceded or not by a pass between the strikers.

2nd situation
The goalkeeper intercedes also at the striker's feet.

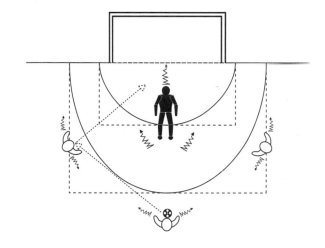

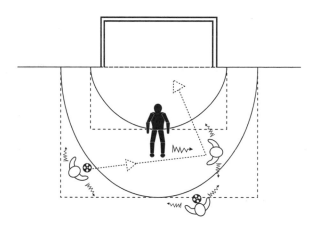

EMPHASIS (points to success)

✳ ✳   Adapt quickly to the situation.
✳ ✳   Remain balanced in all moves.
✳   Carry out the situations at full speed.

GAMES

I INTRODUCTION

THE ACROBAT

Objective   Adapt the run-up and jump according to each situation, taking into account the trajectory of the ball and the position of the striker.

Organization
- Two goals 6 yds wide and two goalkeepers.
- Two strikers each positioned in the opposing 6 yd box
- A field :10 yds wide and 20 yds long.

Development   The goalkeeper with the ball must make a high throw for the striker positioned in the opposing 6 yd area to head the ball and score.

The opposing goalkeeper tries to intercept the ball before the striker (run-up and jump on a single foot or both feet depending on the situation).

After catching the ball, the goalkeeper throws it back to his own striker.

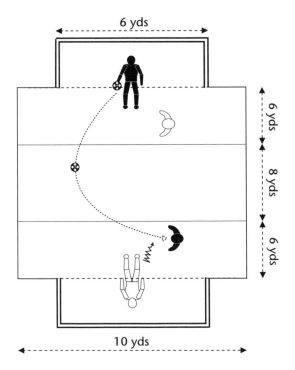

N.B. This game can also apply to high catches.

Count the number of goals scored after a given time.

70

II IMPROVEMENT

THE PRESERVE

Objective   Use any moves necessary in a more pressurized game situation, including active strikers.

Organization • In a center circle, a 6 yd goal with two sides.
  • One goalkeeper in the goal defending both sides.
  • Two teams of three players :
    • Two players outside the center circle (forbidden entrance).
    • One player in the center circle (forbidden exit).

Development Both teams try to score in both goals, with low or high passes, using their striker positioned in the center circle.

The goalkeeper intervenes as soon as the ball enters the center circle (striker against striker and striker (s) against goalkeeper).

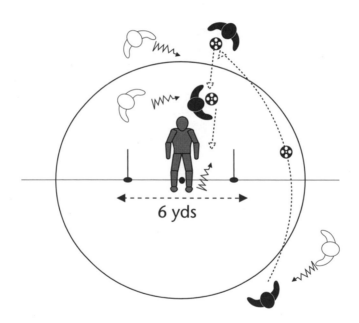

6 yds

Count the number of goals scored by each team at the end of the time of play.

III TRAINING

OVERHEAD TACKLE

Objective   Use all moves necessary in a worked out game session (center and overhead games) including strikers and defenders.

Organization • A field, 20 yds by 18 yds long.
               • Two goalkeepers.
               • Four field players (two strikers against two defenders)
               • Two neutral players, positioned on the wings.

Development The goalkeeper throws the ball back to one of the neutral players who stand outside the field of play at the midfield line. The neutral player plays a high ball into the strikers who play against two defenders and the goalkeeper.

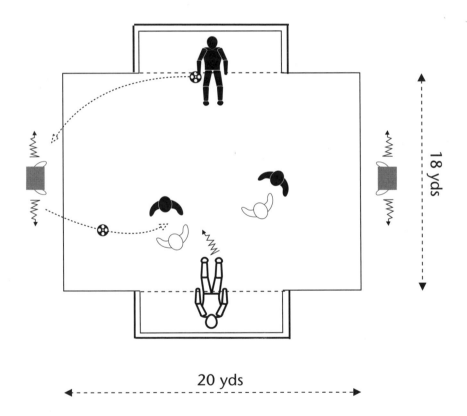

N.B. This game may apply for overhead catches.

Count the number of goals scored by each team in a given time.

72

MASTERING THE BODY

When the ball travels within the penalty area, the goalkeeper is constantly subject to stress due to the high density of players in his area and the aggressiveness of the opposition.

He must therefore, both on the ground and in the air, remain clear-headed for his interventions, despite loss of balance and the distraction or contacts caused by the sudden presence of the opposition.

Mastering his landing will enable him not only to avoid injuries but also to reposition himself always facing the ball, in order to intervene again.

These driving perceptions will be acquired all the more quickly since this specific coaching will be initiated at a young age (11-12 years old).

Thus, the goalkeeper will be able to move in his area with complete confidence.

We will, therefore, study the Mastering of the body:

On the ground and in the air   74 to 78

MASTERING THE BODY

I INTRODUCTION

Objective Basic gymnastic movements.

Organization Use a foam carpet, a sandpit or soft ground.
  Note: **Safety is important**! The coach needs, therefore, to make sure that the moves are appropriate to the various situations.

1st situation
- FORWARD ROTATION OF THE BODY (roll).
- Begin in a crouching position.
- Two footed push off, forward roll.
- Stand without help from the hands.

2nd situation
- BACKWARD ROTATION OF THE BODY (roll).
  - Begin, crouching.
  - Backward shift of balance, on line roll.
  - Back on your feet (dynamic attitude).

3rd situation
- JUMPS
  - Vary the take off.
  - Reduced run-up and a one or two foot take off.

4th situation
- SUPPORT/STRETCH/BACKWARD TILT.
  - Lay the stomach on a high back in order to position the pelvis vertically.
  - (Arms-shoulders-pelvis aligned).

Variation
- Identical to the fourth, include a leg throw, bracing the body in order to land on a padded mat, flat on the back.

EMPHASIS (points to success) ————————————————————

FORWARD ROLL
- Avoid shifting the feet when beginning.
- Land on the arms (shock absorbers) with round back and head bent.
- Stand without the hands touching the ground.
- Land on the soles of your feet (heels off the ground), legs slightly apart.
- Look straight ahead (and not at your feet).
- Place the hands in a catching position.

BACKWARD ROLL
- Link nape and neck to roll in order to avoid falling on the shoulder.
- Place the hands at ear level (thumbs towards the head).
- Use your hands to stand up then place them in a catching position.

JUMPS
- Increase the speed of approach.
- Land on one or both feet.
- Protect the pelvis constantly.
- Co-ordinate the arm-leg movement.
- Look straight ahead.

SUPPORT/STRETCH/BACKWARD TILT

- Position the pelvis, hold in the stomach, tense the buttocks.
- Arms extended (look between your hands).
- Land on the mat, keeping the body stiff.

N.B. SAFETY: The coach is positioned on the side:
- one hand on the nape of the neck
- one hand supports the movement either at back or leg level

II IMPROVEMENT

Objective Combine various movements and increase the time in the air. Include a ball.

Organization A mini-springboard and trampolines.

1st situation FORWARD ROTATION (roll).
• Reduced approach (3 yds).
• Two foot take off on the mini-springboard.
• Lifted roll.
• Landing on the mat.

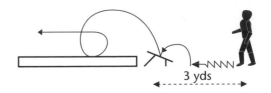

Variation A: Identical to the first situation but with a ball held with both hands or thrown at the moment of the jump.
B: Identical to the first situation but with a ball thrown as soon as the landing has been carried out (link a catch or a dive).

2nd situation BACKWARD ROTATION (roll).
• Begin with straight legs.
• Backward shift of balance.
• Roll and stand.

Variation • Ball held with both hands.
• Ball thrown after the landing.

3rd situation JUMP.
On the springboard:
A combination of jumps (feet together-one foot-both feet).

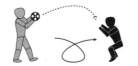

Variation • Ball held with both hands
• Ball thrown after landing on the high block.

4th situation SUPPORT/STRETCH/BACKWARD TILT.
• Begin with legs apart
• Tilt the pelvis
• Master the SSB against a wall.
(legs apart and only one heel against the wall).

EMPHASIS (points to success) ————————————————

FORWARD ROTATION

- Increase the height of the jump with a skilled two-foot take off.
- High roll = time in space (neither hands nor feet touch the ground).
- Land on the arms (shock absorbers).
- Roll over then stand, well-balanced and ready for the next move.

BACKWARD ROTATION

- After the backward shift of balance, absorb the fall by placing the hands along the side of the body.
- Maintain body balance when landing in order to intervene on a thrown ball.

JUMP

- Permanently protect the pelvis to increase the range of each jump.
- Land, body braced, on each springboard.

SUPPORT/STRETCH/BACKWARD TILT

- Take a slight run up to heighten the pelvis and the legs.
- Master the positioning against the wall.
- Arms remain well stretched (hands turned slightly outwards).

III TRAINING

Objective   A study of gymnastic moves including a variety of throws.

Organization Use a mini-springboard.

1st situation   FORWARD ROLL
- Reduced run up (5 yds)
- Two foot take off on a mini-spring-board.
- Forward roll onto a padded mat.

Variation
- With a ball held with both hands.
- With a ball thrown after landing.

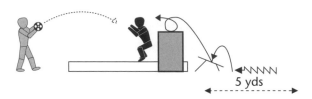

2nd situation   BACKWARD ROTATION
- Begin with run up (backward jump after a backward shift of balance).
- Backward roll on a padded mat;
- Balanced landing.

Variation
- With a ball held with both hands.

3rd situation   JUMP
- Reduced approach.
- Two foot take off on a mini-spring-board.
- Shoulder stand then jump (feet together).

Variation
- After the jump, the server throws a ball towards the goalkeeper, high up in the air. The goalkeeper tries to catch it.

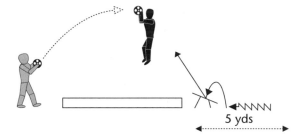

4th situation   SUPPORT/STRETCH/BACKWARD TILT
- Begin with legs apart.
- Temporary support/stretch/backward tilt.
- Landing following a forward roll.
- After the landing, intervention on a thrown ball.

IMPORTANT

The situations above are only offered as complementary information.

They must only be tackled with a coach who has a perfect understanding of the subject, capable of setting up appropriate exercises and likely to intercede efficiently when difficulties arise.

In order to plan this type of session, it is necessary to be surrounded by the appropriate facilities (gymnasium, skirting board, landing mat...........)

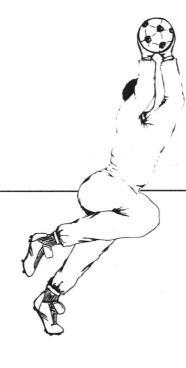

TECHNICAL
PREPARATION

CATCHING THE BALL

During a match, when the goalkeeper **gains possession** of the ball, he **definitely destroys** the opposing offensive action.

He is **master of the game**, and becomes its **first reviver**. He must, therefore, give **priority** to this move, **catch the ball first** and **avoid giving the ball back to the opposition**.

This **intervention** will be particularly subject to **attention** and, in addition to the ground and mid-way catches, the emphasis will be put on **high throws and catches**.

Indeed, there is **no doubt that a goalkeeper who masters his overhead game will relieve his partners** when in pressing situations and will **reassure them throughout the match**.

We will, therefore, study:
- Ground catch   83
- Half-way catch   87
- High catch   91
- Games   95

CATCHING THE BALL ON THE GROUND

I INTRODUCTION

Objective   Break down of the body movement, at a standstill and in slow motion (lateral then forward move).

Organization   Two goalkeepers (alternately: one server; the other goalkeeper). Use of cones or poles to mark the distance which separates the goalkeepers.

1st situation	A server and a goalkeeper, face to face, at 5 yds. The server hand-throws the ball along the ground, towards the goalkeeper who picks it up, flexing the right then the left leg. • Lower the torso to bring the arms nearer the ground. • Slightly lift the knee; it must not touch the ground.
2nd situation	Identical to the first but the ball is thrown at 1 yd, alternately, to the right then to the left of the goalkeeper. The goalkeeper is obliged to "drag-step" before flexing and picking the ball up.
3rd situation	Two goalkeepers face to face, at 5 yds. Each goalkeeper throws his ball towards the cone placed on his right hand side and moves to catch the ball which is thrown towards his left (bend the suitable leg); he then continues running after catching the ball and positions himself behind the cone previously deserted by the other goalkeeper. Exercise to be carried out right and left.

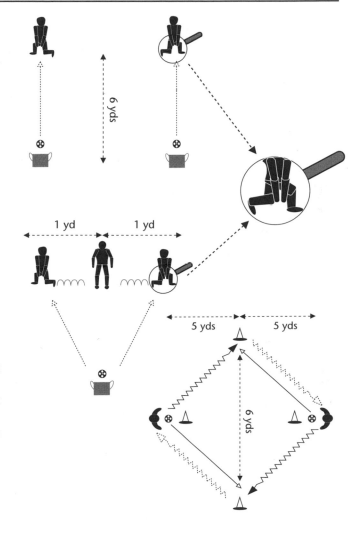

EMPHASIS (points to success)

✶ ✶ ✶   Flex one leg on the opposite heel (the leg is in the way of the trajectory of the ball) the knee must not touch the ground; the trajectory of the ball is between the legs.
   • If the ball lands to the right of the goalkeeper = Flex the right leg.
   • If the ball lands to the left of the goalkeeper = Flex the left leg.

✶ ✶ ✶   Strike the ball forward (think ahead) in order to cut its trajectory (the knee must not touch the ground).

✶ ✶   Position the body behind the ball, then lift it between your feet, hands open facing it; knees apart, arms in, elbows tight (cage). Do not block the ball with your hands, bring them forward towards the ball so that it rolls into your hands and onto your arms, then bring it to your chest.

✶ ✶   Close the cage, bringing your hands towards your chest and lowering your head.

II IMPROVEMENT

Objective Combine the catching of the ball (facing right then left) with accelerated rhythm and include a moderate opposition.

Organization Use cones to replace the goal, then the penalty area and finally the goal area.

1st situation Begin behind the goal.
The server throws the ball along the ground, alternating right and left.
The goalkeeper moves then picks the ball up in front of the cone.
He will reposition himself at the level of the rear cone with dragging-steps (remain facing the game).
Hand throw then kick the ball.

2nd situation A striker drives the ball, beginning at a cone.
The goalkeeper moves towards him and picks the ball up (the supporting foot near the ball). He then clears the ball straight away in order to avoid contact while the striker races straight ahead.

Important The goalkeeper intervenes when the striker has lost the ball and frees himself to the side corresponding to the forward moving leg (left on the diagram).

3rd situation Servers, positioned on the main line and on the wings, kick the balls to the ground and into the goal.
Within the 6 yd area the strikers move in the way of the goalkeeper (no interception). If at all possible, the goalkeeper picks the balls up without diving (goal 4 yds long and 18 +inches high).

N.B. Adapt the goal area to the level of the goalkeeper (2 to 4 yds)

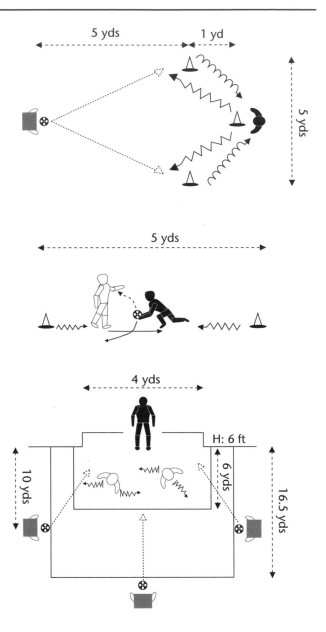

EMPHASIS (points to success)

✳ ✳ ✳ Choose carefully when flexing the legs: this movement should correspond to the drop of the ball.

✳ ✳ Catch the ball fast in order to avoid the dive or contact with the opponent.

✳ ✳ Coordinate the reflex movements (combine moving and catching the ball).

III TRAINING

Objective   A combination of moves carried out at real speed with dynamic oppositions.

Organization Initially, use cones to outline the playing area, then use a mini-goal (height 18 inches) and then the penalty area.

1st situation Two goalkeepers against two other goalkeepers.
A "10 pass" (balls hand-thrown to the ground) in a limited space (5 by 5 yds).

2nd situation A goalkeeper is positioned 2 yds from a mini-goal (width: 1 yd).
A striker is positioned at 5 yds from the mini-goal.
a) The striker pushes the ball in front of him (starter).
b) When the ball is on its way, the goalkeeper positions himself as quickly as possible in his goal area.
c) The striker shoots at ground level into the goal and the goalkeeper intercedes.

3rd situation A goalkeeper defends a goal (width: 2 yds, height: 18 inches) in the 6 yd area.
(No other players may enter this area). Two teams (two against two), in the penalty area try to score. After catching the ball, the goalkeeper throws it back into an unoccupied space in the penalty area.

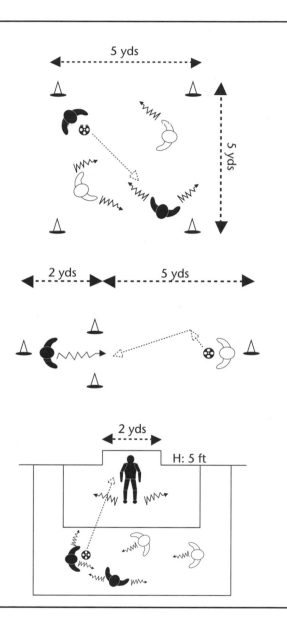

EMPHASIS (points to success)

✳ ✳ ✳   Respect the technique adapted to all situations of the game (i.e.: flexing a leg or returning the ball to the goal cage).

✳ ✳ ✳   Avoid diving when catching the ball is possible.

✳ ✳   Do not hesitate to protect the whole of the body when catching the ball (stomach and pelvis flat on the ground, legs extended and slightly apart for better stability).

✳   Include speed of movement with the catch of the ball.

HALF-WAY CATCH

I INTRODUCTION

Objective   Break down of the movement at a standstill, then moving (facing and lateral).
Insist on the quality of the throw (not too high, not too low).

Organization Two players. Cones.

1st situation Two goalkeepers facing each other, 5 yds away.
One of them hand-throws the ball (at pelvis level). The other catches the ball in the basket shaped by the arms tight against the body, the torso and the head.

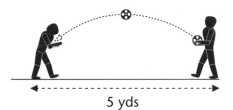

5 yds

2nd situation Two goalkeepers facing each other at 3 yds away from each other and out of line.
They throw the ball in front of them at the same time, then move with fencing steps to catch the other ball.
(exercise to be carried out right then left).

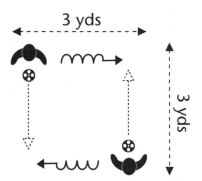

3 yds

3 yds

3rd situation Two goalkeepers positioned 10 yds from each other (one at each cone).
The server hand-throws a straight ball to the ground, the goalkeeper masters the ball after the bounce.

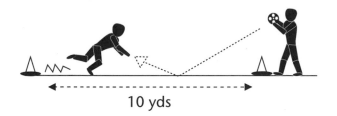

10 yds

EMPHASIS (points to success)

✳ ✳   Position the whole of the body behind the ball.

✳ ✳ ✳   Lower or lift the pelvis depending on the height of the ball.
(if the ball is too high, change the catch)

✳ ✳   Catch the ball at forearm level, the hands must not touch the ball.

✳ ✳   At the end of the catch, the basket is well shaped; arms, torso and head, elbows tight against the body.

II IMPROVEMENT

Objective   Include various movement and one or more moderate oppositions within the exercises.

Organization Use cones then the penalty area and a mini-goal.

1st situation   The server throws the ball half way up into the air and follows its trajectory at a run.
The goalkeeper moves forward, blocks the ball, and frees himself to avoid the opponent positioned at his forward leg.

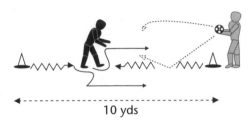

10 yds

2nd situation   Two goalkeepers side by side, at 3 yds from each other.
As soon as the ball is thrown by a server, begin a duel situation, goalkeeper against goalkeeper (shoulder to shoulder contact possible).
Direct hand throw, then hit the ball on the bounce, then "bell shape".

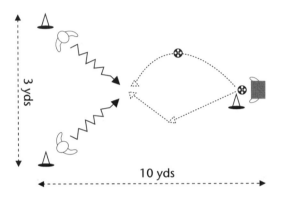

3 yds

10 yds

3rd situation   Strikers, positioned in the 18 yd area (each with a ball), drive the ball towards the goal.
In the 6 yd area, an opponent stands in the way of the goalkeeper without touching the ball (screen).
Height of the goal:
1.5 yds width: 2 yds

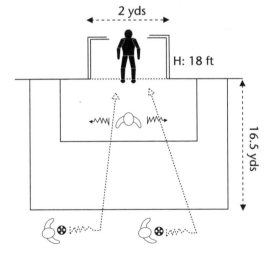

2 yds

H: 18 ft

16.5 yds

EMPHASIS (points to success)

✳ ✳ ✳   A quick study of the trajectory of the ball is necessary in order to position the body in behind the ball.

✳ ✳   Swift intervention on short balls (catch the ball before the bounce).

✳ ✳   Adapt the catch to the trajectory of the ball.

III TRAINING

Objective   A sequence of various moves and half-way catches, despite one or more opponents and a real game.

Organization   Use cones then the penalty area (6 yds and 18 yds).

1st situation   The goalkeeper touches a cone then skirts around an opponent to catch the ball thrown by the latter.

    N.B.   The server throws the ball (direct then rebound) as soon as the goalkeeper touches the cone.

2nd situation   Sequence of four kicks.
The shooters are positioned around the penalty area. Two strikers act as screens in the 6 yd area and intercede if the ball is released by the goalkeeper.
• numbered shots.
• free shots.

    N.B.   The second shot is prompted when the goalkeeper positions himself on his goal line.

3rd situation   The goalkeeper, positioned in the 6 yd area, must intercede on any balls thrown in the 3 yd wide lane, before or after control by the striker.

    N.B.   The servers hand-throw then kick the balls at mid height.

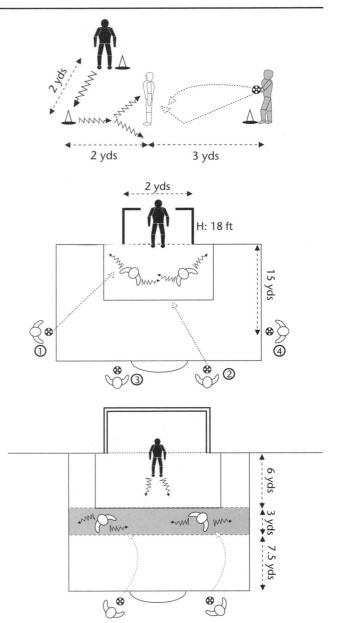

EMPHASIS (points to success)

✳ ✳   In all situations, the combinations must be performed with quality (movements, catching the ball).

✳ ✳   Eliminate apprehension linked to the opponent.

✳ ✳   Very short time between the information (kicking the ball) and the implementation of the movement (choose well when catching the ball).

HIGH CATCH

I INTRODUCTION

Objective   Great care is to be taken as to the quality of the moves.
Insist on carrying out the exercises at a standstill, always beginning with the basic position.
Frequent manipulations of the ball will generate maximum skill.

Organization Use a good leather ball.

1st situation   Bounce the ball with both hands, on your own: In front of you, to the sides, and behind you.

2nd situation   Two goalkeepers face each other at 5 yds
a) One-handed exchange of ball (right and left) above the head.

5 yds

b) Identical to a) but catch the ball with one hand at pelvis level, pass the ball behind the back, change hands then throw.

c) The server kicks the ball, (volley or half volley) at head level of the goalkeeper. The latter catches the ball with both hands.

5 yds

3rd situation   Two goalkeepers face each other:
a) At 5 yds from each other make simultaneous head level hand-throws of both balls, then side step in order to master the other ball.

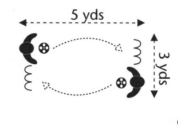

5 yds

3 yds

b) 8 yds away from a server, race 3 yds in order to catch a high ball. The server is the starter of the exercise.

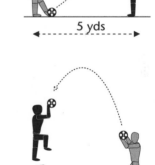

3 yds   5 yds

EMHASIS (points to success)

✳ ✳ ✳   Before the catch, move the body behind the ball (the body is secure).

✳ ✳ ✳   Keep your eye on the ball.

✳ ✳ ✳   Move towards the ball (slight anticipation).

✳ ✳   Having caught the ball, cushion it with the forearms. (forward-backward movement).

✳ ✳ ✳   Cover the ball with your hand with thumbs facing each other.

✳ ✳ ✳   Tighten the elbows when catching the ball with both hands (arms parallel).

✳ ✳ ✳   Simultaneous contact of both hands on the ball (one sound).

✳ ✳ ✳   For a better ambidextrous manipulation, alternate right-hand and left hand exercises.

✳ ✳ ✳   Begin the exercises without gloves in order to feel the ball.

II IMPROVEMENT

Objective A combination of situations in all exercises (link moves/take off: catch/landing).

Organization Cones to outline the goal area.

Remark The server throws the ball high enough in order for the goalkeeper to jump.

1st situation Fencing steps on the goal line.
- To the left = left foot take off.
- To the right = right foot take off.

2nd situation Forward leaning run followed by a catch.
- To the left = right foot take off
- To the right = left foot take off
Repositioning on the goal line, fencing steps, always facing the game.

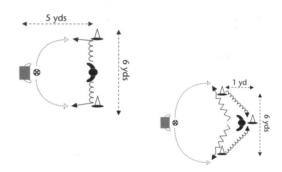

3rd situation **Intervention on a ball thrown on the main line, lobbing the goalkeeper.**
Backward fencing steps.
Take off and landing on backward leg.

N.B. Alternate the position of the right and left leg, backwards.

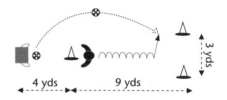

4th situation **Intervention on a ball lobbed to the right then to the left of the goalkeeper.**
Backward slanting run (backward cross-steps).
- To the right = right legged take off, landing on the right leg.
- To the left = left legged take off, landing on the left leg.

N.B. **Once the exercise has been well mastered, in situations numbers 1-4, an opponent may be included, first at a standstill then with a moderate move.**

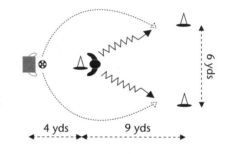

5th situation A server throws a ball at the head of the striker positioned facing the goalkeeper (high ball). The goalkeeper runs, then jumps and catches the ball, avoiding the opponent (to the right or to the left). The opponent is always facing the goalkeeper.

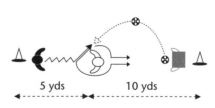

6th situation One goalkeeper against another, side by side.
One of the goalkeepers bounces the ball high up into the air.
1) A is goalkeeper and B remains as a passive, then dynamic opponent.
2) A and B are goalkeepers and both try to catch the ball.

92

EMPHASIS (pedagogical situations of success)

A wrong movement may be generated by a bad implementation of the initial move (see chapter: MOVES).

WORK OF THE LEGS.

Choose the correct take off leg corresponding to the direction of the move.

In order to improve stabilization in the air and protect the body, the free leg must always remain bent and high.

The landing leg must be the same as the take off leg. (no scissors), except in no 1 situation whereby both positions are possible.

WORK OF THE ARMS (see chapter: INTRODUCTION).

Always catch the ball in front of the shoulders in order to retain good balance despite possible contacts (eyes on the ball).

Master the ball as high as possible (arms extended) before bringing it towards the torso (cut out retracting movements).

Always end the situation facing the game: server.

III TRAINING

Objective   Real game situation with varied opposition (teammates-opponents) and the possibility of sequence exercises (i.e.: throw back).

Organization Exercises in the goal area.

1st situation   Duel, one player against another.
The server hand-throws then kicks the ball between two goalkeepers (high and center throw):
1) The goalkeeper who is positioned as an extension of the far post runs forward.
2) The goalkeeper positioned at the near post runs backwards.
(backward cross-steps).
Air duel to catch the ball.

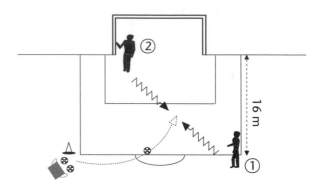

2nd situation   Duel, one player against another.
The server hand throws then kicks the balls into the middle of the goal areas.
Each goalkeeper, in the middle of his goal, intercedes on the high center pass.

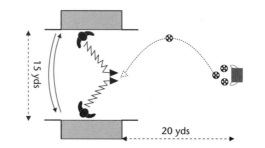

3rd situation   A real game situation with various center passes.
The goalkeeper intervenes despite opponents and partners and follows with a throw back after catching the ball (insist on the ORDER from the goalkeeper).

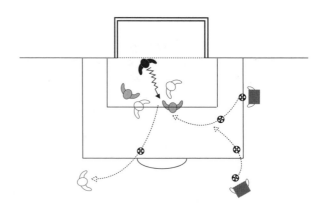

EMPHASIS (points to success)

✳ ✳   Assess the trajectory of the ball.
✳ ✳   Combine catching the ball with a quick throw back in the direction from which it originally came (i.e.: towards a player free from a marker).
✳ ✳ ✳   When center passing, as soon as the ball is on its way, the goalkeeper must always position his torso facing the game.

THE GAMES

I INTRODUCTION

"10" PASS

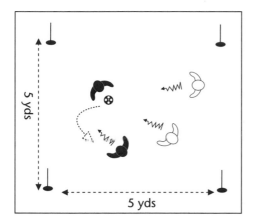

5 yds

5 yds

HEADER

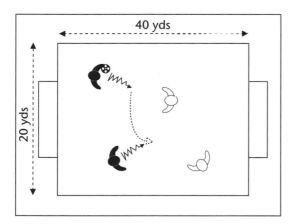

40 yds

20 yds

Objective
Use the appropriate catching techniques.
The quality of the movement must be permanent, despite the opposition (contacts, loss of balance, ...).

Organization
In a square (5 yds), 2 against 2 or 3 against 3, depending upon the number of goalkeepers.

Development
Each team tries to achieve "10" passes consecutively.
The passes are made as follows:

> • free
> • to the ground
> • in the air

Objective
Use the various catching techniques within a traditional collective game, whereby the hands of the goalkeeper replace the feet of the field player (reminder: Basketball).

Organization
A reduced field (minimum 20 by 40 yds).
Vary depending on the number of players.
2 teams of 2, 3 or 4 goalkeepers.

Development
Seek improvement by hand-exchanging balls in order to move closer to the opposite goal and score with the head.
It is compulsory to catch the ball with both hands.
The passes are free (ground, half-way up, high).
Count the number of goals scored.

I INTRODUCTION

TENNIS BALL

Objective
Catches must be adapted to each situation.
The position of the player is privileged and the dive is only used as a last resort.

Organization
An adapted tennis court.
Ground=Variable surface depending on the achievement levels of the interventions.
Height of the net (or fence) = 1.50 yds.
Forbidden area = 3 yds (1.50 yds each side of the net), for the ball and the players.

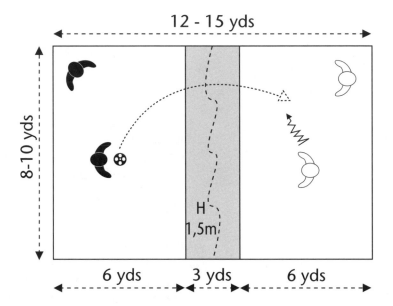

Development
In order to score a point, the ball must touch the ground within the limits of the field without being mastered by the opposite team.
If the ball has been mastered by the opposite team, the bearer of the ball throws it direct or passes it to a better-positioned partner (the bearer of the ball must remain at a standstill).

Variations
1) If the field is wide and not too deep = Favor the lateral move and a catch of ball half way and to the ground (dives are frequent).
2) If the field is not too wide but deep = Favor the lobbed balls = backward moves and high catches.

N.B. To begin with, in order to familiarize the goalkeeper with the game, "high to low" throws are forbidden.
Only seek a low to high movement.

II IMPROVEMENT

THE MAGIC SQUARE

Objective
Combine swiftness with a catching of the ball in order to be able to grab the ball before the opponent.
Guts and will power are a must during the duels.

Organization
Two goalkeepers positioned in a square 5 to 10 yds (dimensions are adapted to the levels of the goalkeepers).
Four servers 8 yds away, positioned facing the four sides of the square.

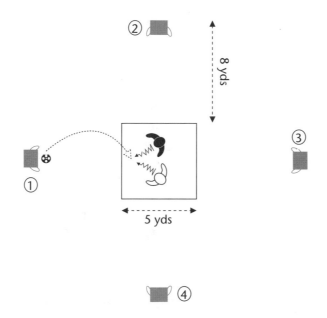

Development
Each server hand-throws a ball in the square.
Duel between both goalkeepers to catch the ball.
The height of the throws are varied (ground level, half-way up, high).
N.B. The servers are numbered and the balls are thrown one after the other
  • either in numerical order: (1-2-3-4) or in any order (2-3-4)

Count the number of balls mastered by each of the goalkeepers after a series of 8 to 12 throws.
Respect the number of catches per series: they will depend on the level of the goalkeepers.

III TRAINING

HIGH DUEL

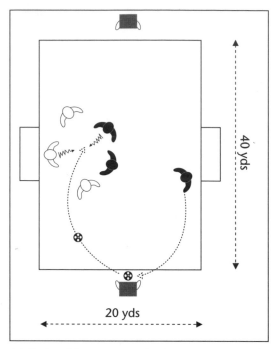

40 yds

20 yds

N.B. In this game, priority is given to the HIGH ball.

THE GUNNERS

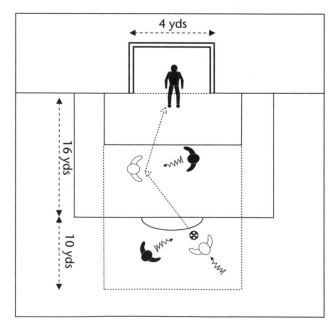

4 yds

16 yds

10 yds

N.B. Note the number of goals scored by each team

Objective
Sharpen the technique of the high catch in a real game.
Master the contacts and the loss of balance.
Position yourself correctly despite the presence of partners and opponents (use of the command).

Organization
A reduced field 40 yds by 20 yds (adapt perimeter to the level of the players).
Two teams of three players each including one goalkeeper and two strikers.
Two neutral players, positioned on the wings, center for the team which hands the ball over to them.

Development
The goalkeeper intercepts the ball on the cross carried out by one of the neutral players then throws it back to the other neutral player positioned to the opposite side from which the ball comes.

Objective
Use any kind of catches on more or less close straight shots.
Try to block the ball first, avoiding a rebound if at all possible.

Organization
One goal area: 4 yds wide (normal height).
Two teams including two field players.
One neutral goalkeeper in the 6 yd area.
One player from each team in the 18 yd area.
One player from each team outside the 18 yd area.

Development
The two teams attack the goal in order to score;
• the players within the 18 yd area must shoot without sense of control,
• the players outside the 18 yd area can only shoot after having caught the ball from the player positioned within the 18 yd area.

THE DIVES

The dive is a spectacular move which excites crowds and flares up the media.

Nevertheless, **the beauty of the move must not be detrimental to its efficiency.** The latter will only be **achieved after intense coaching.**

Having once **mastered the basic movement**, the goalkeeper will be able to include **his personal touch** in each of his interventions.

However, one must never forget **that this move can be dangerous. Indeed, the dive is only the result of poor positioning by the goalkeeper. Thus, this move will only be a compensation.**

It is up to the goalkeeper to choose his style of intervention, never to forget **that diving is useless when movement is feasible.**

We will, therefore, study the dives:

LATERAL DIVES
Right and Left

INTRODUCTION

Objectives   Coaching the quality of the move, giving priority to security in landing and with a view to efficiency.

Organization First use a sand pit, then soft ground (grass).
Protect the knees with pads.

1st situation Begin kneeling then fall laterally, moving the pelvis sideways.
• Without a ball, arms bent, hands forward.
• Holding a ball.
• Throwing a ball at shoulder level, then to the ground (20 inches right then left of the goalkeeper).

2nd situation Identical to the first, but begin in a squat position.

At a standstill a) Move the pelvis sideways then fall laterally.
(b) Lateral start then sideways movement of the pelvis, then fall.

3rd situation In a sand pit.
A server holds the ball with one hand, mid-air.
To begin with, the goalkeeper squats then grabs the ball following a push off the outward leg (do not fall).
Exercise to be carried out right then left.
Same situation to be carried out in a standing position.

4th situation The goalkeeper begins inside the goal area (at 0.50 yds from the goal line and at 2 yds from the post).
The server throws the ball towards a post.
The goalkeeper dives laterally, cutting the trajectory of the ball and grabbing it in front of the post.
Repeat the exercise to the right then to the left.
Ground then mid-air throws.

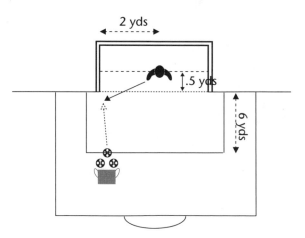

EMPHASIS (points to success)

✳✳✳   Always keep an eye on the ball.

✳✳✳   Catch the ball in front (arms must not be trapped to your sides).

✳✳✳   Contact with the ground must be with the foot, then the thigh, the side and finally the arms.

✳✳✳   Fall on your side and not on your back or stomach.

✳✳   Round falls to the ground only.

✳✳✳   The ball must avoid contact with the ground.

✳✳✳   Keep the body between the ball and the goal (remain facing the game). Lock the pelvis.

✳✳✳   Try to cut off the trajectory of the ball.

II IMPROVEMENT

Objectives Vary the combinations (a movement followed by a dive or a right or left hand dive).

Organization Choose soft ground and the goal area.

1st situation A combination of movements followed by a dive. To begin with, the goalkeeper is lying on his side.
a) the server throws the ball into the hands of the goalkeeper,
b) the goalkeeper catches it, throws it back to him, and immediately raises himself up slightly (use of the hand on the ground).

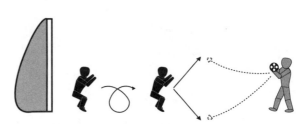

Then, falling laterally, he pushes himself with his outward leg in order to intercept the same ball thrown further away.
Link several dives to the right then to the left.

Important The push off leg (outward leg) is always crossed forward.

2nd situation A combination of forward rolls followed by a dive.
The goalkeeper begins in his goal area with his feet together. Forward roll and landing on the soles of the feet, hands forward.
After having stabilized his supports, he dives on the ball thrown mid height by the server positioned to his right or to his left.

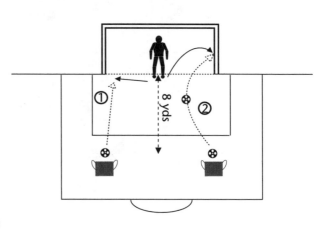

3rd situation A combination of dives in the goal area. A server hand-throws a first ball to the ground to one side of the goal.(1) The goalkeeper dives, stops the ball, stands up, then intercepts the second ball thrown mid height to the opposite side by the server.(2)
Begin the exercise on the right side then on the left side of the goal.

Variation Throw the first ball mid height, then the second ball to the ground.

4th situation A combination of rolls in the goal followed by a ninety-degree turn and return to dive.
To begin with (facing the opposite post) the goalkeeper carries out a forward roll, then a ninety-degree turn to stand and face the game and intercepts a ball thrown in front of a cone situated 1 yd from the post, by the starter of the exercise (apply the correct techniques).

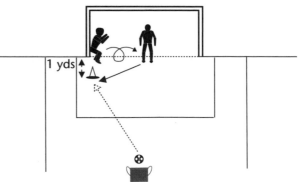

Variation Begin the exercise with a backward roll.

102

EMPHASIS (points to success)

✳✳✳ Keep both feet on the ground (with the exception of the heels) and the body in basic position when throwing or catching the ball.

✳✳✳ Push off your feet when diving. Do not just fall to the ground.

✳✳✳ Pay attention to the force of the **MOVEMENT**. Allow for the physical recovery of the goalkeeper in all situations.

III TRAINING

Objectives Master the technique of all situations of the game. Include partners and opponents.

Organization Use of the goal area and the penalty area.

1st situation Subject: A combination of body building relaxation followed by a dive.
The goalkeeper jumps laterally with both feet over a low fence: he then lands on both feet and dives (in front of a cone), cutting the trajectory in order to intercept the kick.
Repeat the exercise 5 to 10 times.

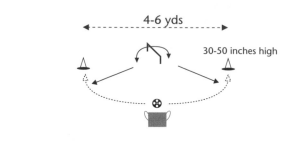

Variation Bending under the fence (height: approx: 1 yd)
Bend the legs maintaining a straight torso, eyes on the ball.

Important After each shot, the goalkeeper side steps to position himself with his body facing the game.

2nd situation A goalkeeper is positioned at the near post.
Intervention (1) on a cross (straight ball) then repositioning (2) in front of the goal and dive (3) on the second ball (right then left exercise).

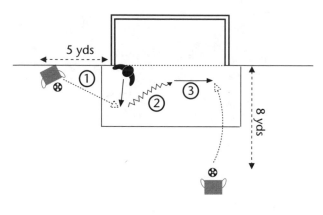

3rd situation A goalkeeper in the goal area.
Movement within an area (width: 1 yd) and intervention on shots coming from the 18 yd area.
One or two strikers, at a standstill or moving, screen the goalkeeper and pounce on any rebounds.

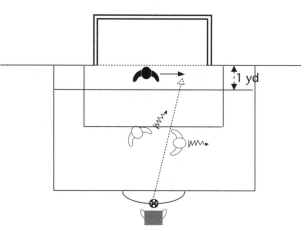

EMPHASIS (points to success)

✳✳✳ Choose the correct take off leg for the dive (see following page).
✳✳✳ Try to block the ball (use both hands) before diverting it if necessary.
✳✳ Link the quality of the movement with efficiency.

IMPORTANT

Remember that the dive is only the **CONSEQUENCE** of a **DELAYED ACTION** from the goalkeeper when **POSITIONING** himself during an intervention.

The dive is, therefore, only a compensatory move.

Two possibilities may apply:

1) Intervention on a HIGH BALL (below the cross bar)
• Push off the **INWARD** Leg
i.e.: if the ball is **LEFT** of the goalkeeper, Push off the LEFT leg.

• **PRIORITY** is given to the use of the hand corresponding to the side of the dive, keeping the option open to use the **OPPOSITE HAND** on balls situated below the cross bar.
i.e.: Use the right hand for a left dive

2) Intervention on a LOW BALL
• Push off the **OUTWARD** leg
i.e.: if the ball is **LEFT** of the goalkeeper, push off the **RIGHT** leg.

• **PRIORITY** is given to the hand corresponding to the side of the dive.
i.e.: Use the left hand for a left dive

N.B. Differentiation
"High ball" and "Low Ball"

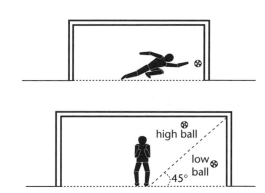

REMINDER

High Ball = **Push off inward leg.**
Low Ball = **Push off outward leg.**

FORWARD DIVES

INTRODUCTION

Objectives   Learn the quality of the movements, prioritizing safety when landing with a view to efficiency. (see "Introduction to lateral dives").

Organization   Identical to lateral dives but insist on prioritizing the protection of the elbows.

1st situation   Begin kneeling, fall forward and land on the forearms.
a) with a ball held in the cradle formed by your arms.
b) with a ball thrown 50 yds in front of the goalkeeper (at torso level).

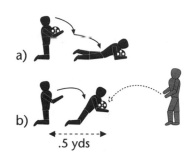

.5 yds

2nd situation   Identical to the first, but begin the exercise squatting.
• at a standstill.
• after a forward jump.

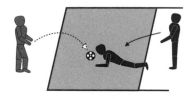

3rd situation   In a sand pit.
A ball is thrown in front of the goalkeeper who is in a standing position. He propels himself forward (no fall) and grabs the ball.
The throws must be further and further away from the goalkeeper (efficient push of the legs).

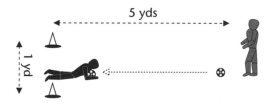

4th situation   On a ball thrown to the ground (straight shot) in a mini-goal 1 yd wide, the goalkeeper blocks the ball with the pelvis pinned to the ground (protection).

5 yds

1 yd

EMPHASIS (points to success)

✳✳✳   Pick the ball up within the cradle formed by the forearms, before lying down.
The first contact with the ground is a foot contact.
✳✳✳   Pin the pelvis to the ground, legs wide apart (better stabilization) in order to protect the ball.
✳✳✳   Sheathe the body to cushion the fall.
✳✳   Reminder of the techniques for catching the ball on the ground.

II IMPROVEMENT

Objectives   Apply the technique in a game situation. Include opponents.

Organization   Use soft ground to cushion the fall of the goalkeeper.

1st situation   The striker dribbles the ball towards the goalkeeper.
The goalkeeper runs, picks the ball up and frees himself very quickly (the striker is very aggressive) to the right or to the left, then dives forward.

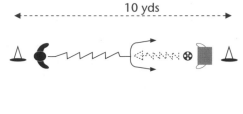

2nd situation   A striker faces the goalkeeper at 3 yds. The server throws a ball with a slight bounce towards the right or towards the left of the striker.
As soon as the ball is thrown, the goalkeeper moves forward, grabs the ball then falls to the ground to protect it.

EMPHASIS (points to success)

✳✳✳   Choose the correct foot to clear in order to avoid the pressing opponent.
• for a left clearance = bring the left foot forward.
• for a right clearance = bring the right foot forward.

✳✳   Guts and willpower in the intervention.
✳✳   Be sure of your decision.

III TRAINING

Objectives Real game situation, remain clear-headed in the intervention despite opponents.

Organization Use the goal area and the penalty area.

1st situation Alternately, the goalkeeper defends two mini-goals, 1 yd wide each, ground shooting only.
He intervenes on the first shot, turns round and positions himself in the second mini-goal to stop the second shot and so on (intense rhythm).
A series of five consecutive interventions.

N.B. The second server shoots while the goalkeeper repositions himself.

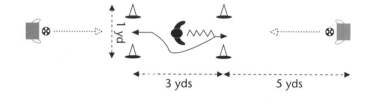

2nd situation The goalkeeper defends a goal, 2 yds wide, on flat shots kicked by a server positioned at 9 yds
A striker positioned at a minimum of 3 yds from the goal disturbs the goalkeeper (without touching the ball) and intercepts any rebounds.

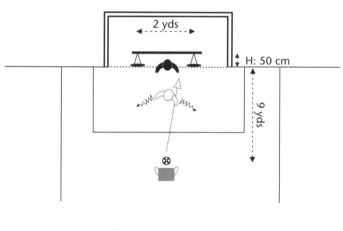

3rd situation A server positioned on the main line or on the wings shoots flat between the striker and the goalkeeper.
As soon as the ball is kicked, tackle one on one.
The goalkeeper intercedes by grabbing the ball and freeing himself quickly.
The striker tries to score a goal.

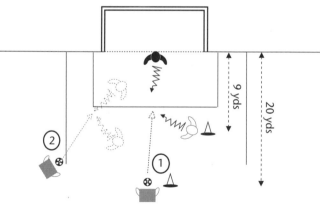

EMPHASIS (points to success)

✳✳ High speed is necessary in order to avoid the opponent.
✳✳ Decide quickly.
✳✳ Courage in all tackles.

N.B. Exercises are to be frequently carried out on damp ground (skipping ball).

DIVES BACKWARD

INTRODUCTION

NOTE:
It is indeed essential to master beforehand:
Backward and forward: slanting moves
Ground landings when diving backwards or forwards in order to reduce the risks in trauma, which would be harmful to the healthy progression of the goalkeeper.

✳ ✳ ✳

II IMPROVEMENT

Objectives   Break down the move with maximum SECURITY, improving the ground landing (fall). Revision of the objectives which have already been studied in the chapter "Lateral dives".

Organization   Use a sand pit.

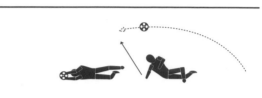

1st situation   On a slow lobbed ball thrown to the right then to the left.
When the ball is being thrown, the goal-keeper, who is sitting down, stands up slightly and propels himself backwards using the outward leg.
He lands on his side after having blocked the ball.

Important   • Right intervention = Push off the left leg.
• Left intervention = Push off the right leg.

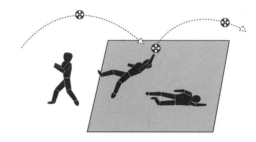

2nd situation   The goalkeeper stands in profile to the server and on the edge of a sand pit.
On a low lobbed ball, he propels himself with the backward leg and uses the corresponding arm to deflect the ball away from the sand pit.
He lands on his side, arm extended.

Important   • **Right side**
Push off the right foot = Deflect with the right hand
• **Left side**
Push off the left foot   = Deflect with the left hand

Variation   Same situation, only the goalkeeper blocks the ball.

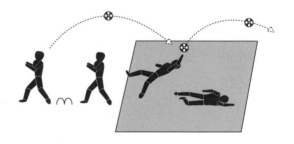

3rd situation   Identical to the second, only the intervention is preceded by two backward slanting steps (fencing steps) before diving.

Variation   It is possible to use the backward crossed step.

EMPHASIS (points to success)

✳✳✳   Choose the correct take off leg and the corresponding arm in order to deflect the ball.
✳✳   Keep your eyes on the ball.
✳✳✳   Land on your side (see technique of the lateral dive).
✳✳✳   Eliminate any apprehension you have of the fall (confidence).
✳✳✳   Only deflect the ball if absolutely necessary. Indeed, priority must be given to the catching of the ball in all circumstances.

N.B. This technique is only used with fast balls.
The slow lobbed throws only affect the coaching phase, because a fast move should be enough to

III TRAINING

Objectives   In a real game situation, combined moves followed by a backward dive.

Organization   In the goal area and the penalty area.

1st situation   The goalkeeper stands on the main line and at 10 yds from the goal.
On a fast lobbed ball thrown by a server, the goalkeeper steps back, fencer stepping, before diving backwards in order to block or deflect the ball out of the goal.

          a) without opponents.
          b) with opponents acting as a screen.

Carry out the exercises to the right then to the left.

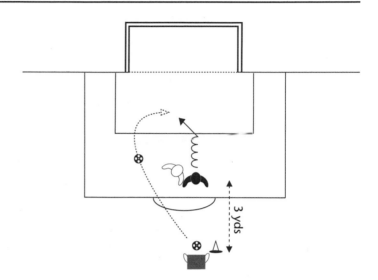

2nd situation   The goalkeeper is positioned at the first post.
On a center lob behind the server (ball thrown towards the far post), the goalkeeper steps back with crossed steps before diving in order to block or deflect the ball.

          a) without opponents.
          b) with opponents acting as a screen.

Carry out the exercises to the right then to the left.

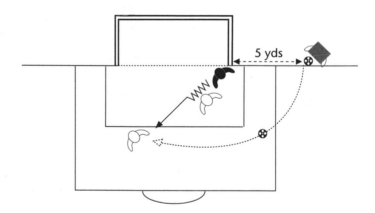

EMPHASIS (points to success)

✳✳✳   If at all possible, avoid diving to catch the ball.
✳✳✳   Choose the correct take off leg and the corresponding arm which will come in contact with the ball (see chapter on backward move; improvement).
✳✳✳   Try to master the ball first before deflecting it.
  ✳✳   A good peripheral eyesight is necessary (ball-partners-opponents).

THE REFLEX MOVE

INTRODUCTION

Objectives   Adapt quickly to fast alternating trajectories of the ball.

Organization   Use a rugby ball, cones and a reduced goal area.

Reminder   Refer to the specific speed exercises adapted to the level of each player (insist on swiftness to the ground).

1st situation   The server kicks the ball on the ground towards a mini-goal (2 yds) using a rugby ball (moderate kicks).
The goalkeeper adapts to the irregular bounces and tries to catch the ball.

2nd situation   The goalkeeper is positioned on his goal line.
The server kicks two balls at the same time.
The goalkeeper reacts depending on the trajectories of the balls and intercepts the first or the second ball (decision of the server).

3rd situation   Grazing shot by the server on obstacles (cones) which will deflect the ball.
The goalkeeper must react to the new trajectories of the ball.

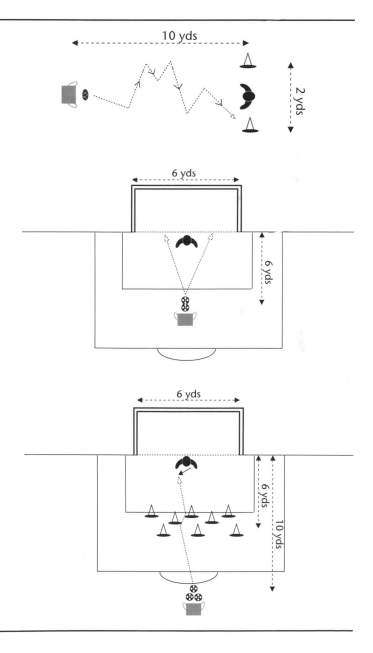

EMPHASIS (points to success)

✳✳   Stand in the way of the ball.
✳✳   React as quickly as possible to irregular trajectories.

II IMPROVEMENT

Objectives   Combine specific speed (movement, reaction, ground swiftness) to an efficient dive depending on an adapted technique.

Organization   Use a goal area, a wall and a soft surface.

1st situation   A server stands behind a goal area, 6 yds wide.
A striker stands 6 yds away from the goal.
The server passes the ball over the goal to the striker, who controls and shoots or sends a header directly on goal.

2nd situation   The goalkeeper faces a wall in a goal area, 6 yds wide. A server is positioned behind the goalkeeper.
The server kicks the ball against the wall, varying the trajectories.
The goalkeeper intercepts immediately after the rebound.

3rd situation   The goalkeeper stands in a mini-goal area (3 yds) and the striker has a foothold on the ball.
As soon as the striker (starter) moves the ball, the goalkeeper moves forward and stabilizes when the ball is kicked in order to intercept the ball by catching it or diving. The striker only moves the ball once.

4th situation   The goalkeeper is positioned at the near post of a reduced goal area (3 yds).
A server stands on the goal line. Two strikers stand in the penalty area. The server passes the ball to one of the strikers who kicks the ball first time on goal.
Reflex-stop of the goalkeeper.
Exercise to be carried out right then left.

EMPHASIS (points to success)

✳✳✳   Stand in the way of the trajectory of the ball.

✳✳✳   Keep both feet on the ground (heels off the ground) when the ball is kicked.

✳✳   Guts and willpower (eliminate apprehension).

III TRAINING

Objectives   In a real game situation increase the screen players, number of balls and opponents.

Organization   In a goal area (reduced in size or not).

1st situation   The goalkeeper is positioned on the main goal line in a mini-goal.
A server, positioned 7 yds from the goal, kicks to score.
One or two strikers in the 6 yd area must avoid or deflect the ball.

2nd situation   The goalkeeper and a screen striker in the 6 yd area.
Three mobile strikers, each with a ball in the 18 yd area, dribble around and one by one shoot at goal.
The goalkeeper intercepts either by deflecting the shot or by catching any ball which has been released.

3rd situation   The server strikes a ball deep within the goal, 5 yds from the striker.
When the ball is on its way:
• The striker sprints and kicks the ball first time on goal.
• The goalkeeper moves out of his goal area and stabilizes himself when the ball is kicked (intercepts by catching the ball or diving,) blocking the ball or deflecting it.

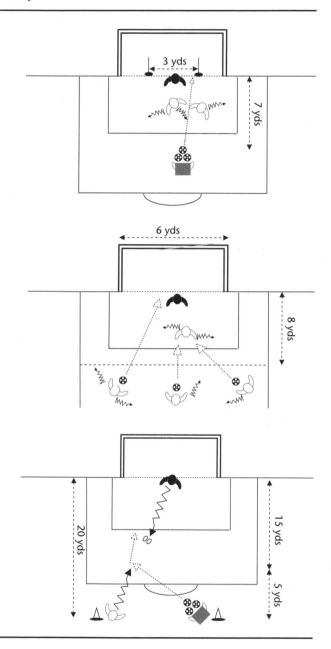

EMPHASIS (points to success)

✳✳✳   During the move and the stabilization of the goalkeeper, the exercise must be carried out at great speed.

✳✳   Use the reduced angle (see page 121).

✳✳   Great concentration in order to react quickly.

✳✳   Push all the kicks (power).

THE GAMES

We suggest 6 games particularly adapted to the dives, but most of the games which are introduced in the other topics may also be carried out.

INTRODUCTION

THE MAGIC SQUARE

Catching the ball *(Improvement)*

Objective
Use any kind of dive in order to protect your square.

Organization
• 1 goalkeeper in a square 8 yds by 8 yds (adapt the perimeter for the goalkeepers at the lowest level).
• 4 servers positioned around the square.

Development
The goalkeeper must intercept all the balls crossing the square.
For mid-air and high balls, intercede before the bounce, if possible.
  • if the goalkeeper blocks the ball = 2 points
  • if the goalkeeper deflects the ball = 1 point

Count the number of points scored by each goalkeeper after each series of eight balls.

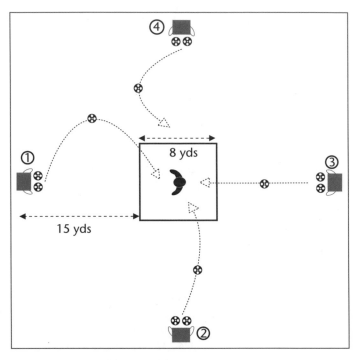

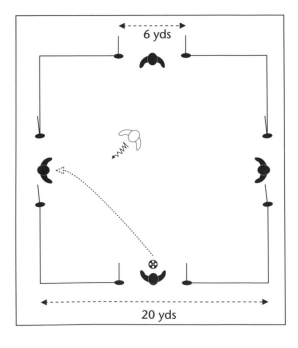

THE KNOCK-OUT

Specific speed *(Introduction)*

Objective
Intervention of the goalkeepers on close and sudden throws or kicks.

Organization
Five goalkeepers:
• Four position themselves in a goal area.
• One acts as striker.

Development
With the ball, the goalkeeper tries to score in one of the three other goals, (hand-throw then kick). The striker intervenes in case the ball is driven back. Switch striker/goalkeeper each time a goal is scored.

Adapt the perimeter to each level.

118

II IMPROVEMENT

TENNIS BALL

Catching the ball *(Introduction)*

Objective
Recover all the balls before they touch the ground in your own area.
The ground surface is adapted to the dives.

Organization
• A ground similar to a tennis court : height of the net 1.5 yds
• A restricted area of 3 yds(i.e. 1.5 yds each side of the net).
Two teams including one or two goalkeepers.

Development
A goalkeeper hand-throws a ball in one of the free spaces without entering his restricted area (he may throw the ball in the restricted area belonging to the opponent).
As soon as the ball is mastered:
2 possibilities:
    a) direct throw, at a standstill.
    b) a pass to the better positioned partner.

VARIATION: A dominant reflex-move *(swiftness on the ground)*.
Organization: The net is replaced by a mini-fence 20 inches high.
Development: The striker kicks the ball under the fence
(grazing kick) in order to score in the goal at the end of the field.

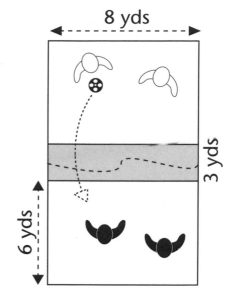

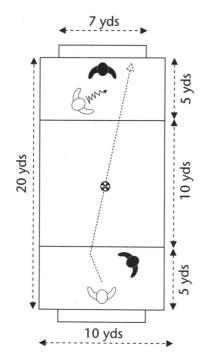

FACE TO FACE

Objective
Intervention on straight kicks despite a striker.
Organization: 2 teams including 2 goalkeepers
• Two move in the goal area
• Two act as strikers

Development
Each goalkeeper tries to score in the opposite goal from his 5 yd area.
The striker stands in the way of the opposite goalkeeper and grabs the ball if released.
Exchange of striker/goalkeepers after a series of ten kicked balls (five for each team).
Count the number of goals scored.

IMPORTANT

It is possible to modify the surface of the field (width and depth) depending on the level of the goalkeepers, who must dive as often as possible.

III TRAINING

THE FORBIDDEN AREA

Objective
Combine replacement with intervention on all kicks.

Organization
A goal , width: 6 yds
A forbidden area: radius: 9 yds (i.e. the center of a field).
A goalkeeper in a goal area which includes two entrances.
Two teams around the restricted area.

Development
The two teams try to score in both sides of the same goal without entering the restricted area. The goalkeeper throws the ball back in a free area.

VARIATION: It is possible to include a player from each team in the restricted area; he may score if the ball is released by the goalkeeper.

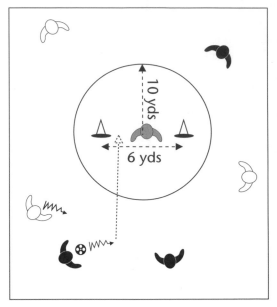

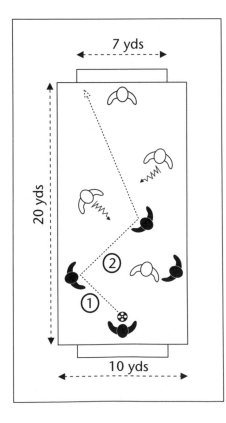

THE GUNNER

Objective
Interception on close kicks despite a great density of players.

Organization
Match in a reduced field *(20 yds by 10 yds)*.
Two teams are present *(2 against 2 and 2 goalkeepers)*.

Development
Each team tries to score in the opposite goal.
A shot is compulsory after a maximum of two passes.
The goalkeeper carries out all his throwbacks by hand.

VARIATION: A game of close scores *(with the field players)*.

Organization
Possibility to use the penalty area *(20 by 40 yds)* with goals 20 yds away.
Two teams *(4 against 4 and two goalkeepers)*.

Development
Each team tries to score in the opposite goal.

120

REDUCING THE SHOOTING ANGLES

In spite of the goalkeeper's physical and technical skills, the efficient interception of all ball trajectories is not possible.

Therefore, he must **move towards the ball** in order to **reduce to a minimum the scoring possibilities of the opponent**, whether the latter's kicks are straight or bending.

The **simple act of moving forward** allows him to **reduce the distance** between himself and the ball and **cut the trajectory of the ball** more easily since he is carrying out a **slightly forward intervention**.

Nevertheless, the goalkeeper must remain aware that as **he moves towards the ball, he becomes vulnerable to the lobbed trajectories**.

We will, therefore, study:

REDUCING THE SHOOTING ANGLE

INTRODUCTION

Objectives   Be aware of the position of the goalkeeper in relation to the goal and the ball.
Slow motion exercise.

Organization Carry out the exercise in the goal and the penalty area.

1st situation   Note the triangle formed at its base by the two posts and at its apex by the ball.
The goalkeeper leaves his goal area, positions himself on the midpoint of the triangle and intercepts the balls kicked along the ground.
The server hits the ball as soon as the goalkeeper is repositioned.
Carry out the exercise facing the goal, then at the two angles of the penalty area.

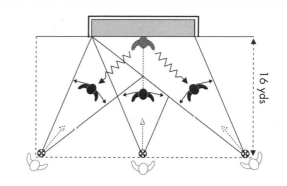

2nd situation   The striker moves parallel to the goal (at the 18 yd line).
The goalkeeper follows the striker, sidestepping, in his 6 yd area, and as he moves he forms the arc of a circle.
If he is too slow, the striker scores a goal.
The exercise is to be carried out to the right then to the left.

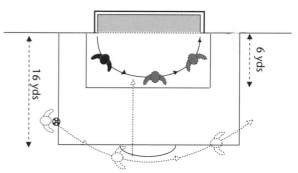

3rd situation   A goalkeeper is positioned on his goal line.
Five balls are aligned in front of him (in the 18 yd area).
The striker chooses his ball and runs to kick.
The goalkeeper positions himself as soon as the ball has been chosen (he moves forward to reduce the angle of the shot, taking into account the imaginary triangle).
After each repetition, the striker chooses another ball.

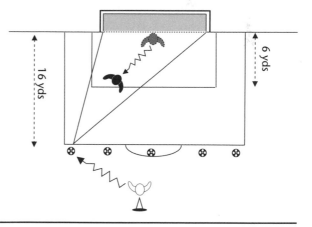

EMPHASIS (points to success)

✳✳✳   The goalkeeper moves forward with the strides preceding the strike
(fast and shorter and shorter strides).

✳✳✳   The goalkeeper must remain stable and balanced at the time of the kick
(support on his feet, heels off the ground).

✳✳✳   Reducing the angle of the shot must be carried out at the last moment in order to avoid
anticipation from the striker (a modification of his first choice, i.e.: lobbed ball).

✳✳   For all lateral moves, use side-steps (the speed of movement will correspond to the
movement of the ball).

II IMPROVEMENT

Objectives   A combination of moves followed by a reduction of the shooting angle.

Organization In the goal area.

1st situation   A goalkeeper in his goal, facing the ball.
Two strikers positioned at both angles of the penalty area.
The first striker moves to the right or to the left and shoots as soon as he has an opportunity (the goalkeeper follows his movement).
As soon as the ball has been shot, the goalkeeper repositions himself in order to intercept on the ball kicked by the second striker.

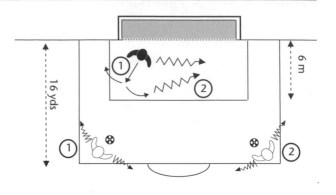

2nd situation A goalkeeper in his goal.
Two strikers in the 18 yd area.
Three possibilities for the striker:
1: A straight shot,
2: A dribble followed by a shot,
3: A pass to his teammate who is positioned on the opposite side of the area, or
A dribble and a pass to his teammate.

Exercises to be carried out to the right then to the left.
The choice of the striker will depend on the position and the movement of the goalkeeper.

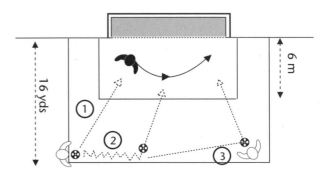

EMPHASIS (points to success)

✳✳✳   Adapt the speed of the goalkeeper to the movement of the ball (grazing side-steps).

✳✳✳   Assess the time to move (when the ball is far from the foot of the striker) and the time to stabilize (when the ball is near the foot of the striker).

✳✳   Keep an eye on the ball.

124

III TRAINING

Objectives   Analyze the particular situations regarding the off-centered balls.

Organization   Use the goal area and the penalty area.

1st situation   The ball is situated near the goal line and the goal.
The striker   1: tries to shoot
                      2: tries to center back
The goalkeeper positions himself 18 inches from the near post.
The interception is possible in both situations.

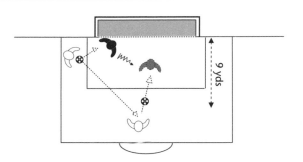

2nd situation   The ball is near the goal line but far from the goal.
The striker carries out:
1: shots at the near post.
2: crossing lobs at the far post.
The goalkeeper positions himself in the middle of the goal to intercept.

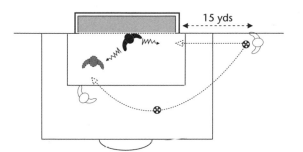

3rd situation   The ball is distant from the goal line and the goal.
The striker carries out:
    1: a direct shot
    2: a long, lobbed cross
The goalkeeper positions himself at 1.5 yds from the first post because:
    • the angle is reduced for the straight shot.
    • Interception on a center pass is possible.

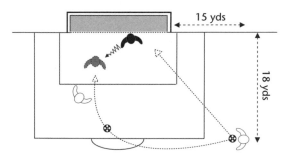

Important: In the 2nd and 3rd situations, the goalkeeper must never be facing the ball or totally facing the game.
It is up to him to compromise in order to intercept efficiently not only the direct kicks at the near post but also the center lobs.

4th situation   The ball is far from the goal line but near the goal. The striker can carry out all direct shots at the near and far post. Therefore, the goalkeeper must reduce the shooting angle but with a slight forward move in order to stop low shots and lobbed chips.

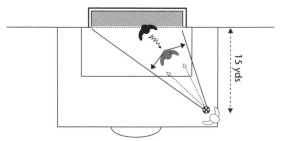

EMPHASIS (points to success)

✱✱✱   Feet must be well positioned (chest facing the ball) in order to intercede in all situations.

✱✱✱   Avoid moving forward too much on bouncing balls, since bounces make it easier for the striker to hit lobbed balls.

THE GAMES

I – INTRODUCTION　　II - IMPROVEMENT　　III - TRAINING

THE "KAMIKAZEE"

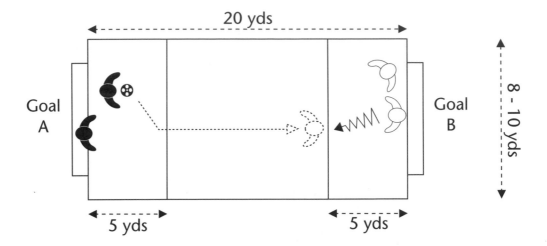

Objective	Efficient intervention on all kicks
Organization	A field 20 yds long and 8 to 10 yds wide. Two kicking areas 5yds wide (adapt the surface and the distance of the game according to the level of the players). In each team; one goalkeeper and one striker.
Development	1) The striker belonging to team A moves the ball in his shooting area (try to gain some ground), before kicking the ball in the opposite goal (the striker only pushes the ball once). 2) The goalkeeper belonging to team B moves forward in order to reduce the shooting angle when the ball is pushed, stabilizing when the striker is about to shoot and intercepts the shot.

Identical exercise to be carried out by the team A goalkeeper and the team B striker.

Reverse roles after 10 shots (Striker-Goalkeeper).

Count the number of goals scored. |

126

DIVE AT THE FEET OF THE OPPONENT

This **move** has the reputation of **being risky** for the goalkeeper.
It therefore requires a goalkeeper with exceptional **moral qualities** (courage-willpower).

In order to restrict the dangers, the choice in triggering the move must be quick and decisive.

Two options result from this choice:
- **direct intervention with the hands on the ball** when the goalkeeper can Take possession of the ball before the opponent.
- **the body (shield) in front of the ball** when the goalkeeper moves at the same time as the opponent

For this intervention, the navel must be centered on the ball, the top half of the body (arms rigid and extended) and the bottom half of the body (legs extended) equally divided as a screen.

In these two fields it is essential to acquire a perfect technique.
Mastering this move will avoid any ambiguity when decisions are to be made by the referee.

We will, therefore, study:

DIVE AT THE FEET

I INTRODUCTION

Objectives To overcome the apprehension of the goalkeeper in relation to the opponent when the goalkeeper is in a seemingly inferior position (lying at the attacker's feet).

Organization Use soft ground (grass or sand).

1st situation A striker dribbles a slow ball in all directions.
The goalkeeper dives:
1) at the feet of the striker, hands on the ball if the ball is distant from the feet of the striker.
2) using his body as a screen, if the ball remains by the feet of the striker.
• As soon as the ball is blocked by the goalkeeper, he releases it, stands up and the exercise begins again; if the ball is deflected, the striker recovers the ball and starts again.

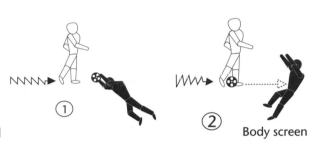

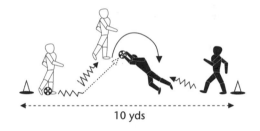
Body screen

2nd situation A striker and a goalkeeper, face to face, 10 yds from each other. As soon as the striker has begun his run (to the right or to the left), the goalkeeper moves forward and dives at his feet (hands on the ball). The striker continues running and jumps over the goalkeeper.

10 yds

3rd situation A striker dribbles a slow ball.
As soon as he has cleared the two cones which are in front of him, he increases his speed, ball at his feet, in order to touch one of the two posts which are positioned to the right or to the left of the goalkeeper. The goalkeeper moves as soon as the striker has cleared the two cones and intercepts with a dive at his feet in order to keep him from touching the chosen post.

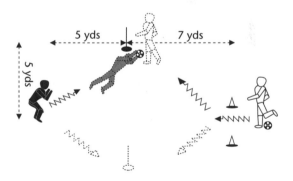
5 yds   7 yds
5 yds

EMPHASIS (points to success)

✳✳✳ Decide on the intervention when the ball has left the feet of the opponent.

✳✳ Move quickly from the standing position to the lying position.

✳✳✳ Choose the correct side of the body to lie down:
   • Ball to the right = lie on the RIGHT side.
   • Ball to the left = lie on the LEFT side.

✳✳ Dive 1.5 yds to 2 yds away from the opponent and finish off sliding, centering the ball on the navel.

✳✳ Arrive at the same time as the foot of the opponent in order to avoid a clash.

✳✳✳ Do not attack the ball with the feet.

✳✳ Repeat the situations often in order to suppress apprehension.

II IMPROVEMENT

Objectives   A combination of a run-up followed by reducing the shooting angle and intervention at the feet.

Organization Exercise to be carried out in the goal.

1st situation   A striker is positioned at 18 yds in a corridor formed with cones: width 3 yds.
A goalkeeper is positioned at the opposite end of the corridor.
In the corridor, the striker must dribble as quickly as possible to the goal line.
The goalkeeper moves when the striker begins his run (starter) and lies on the ball, cutting its trajectory.
The exercise is to be carried out to the right and to the left.

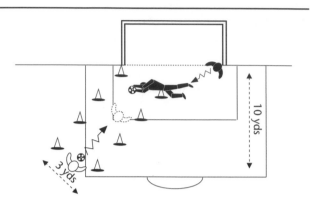

2nd situation   Forward movement of a striker who dribbles the ball SLOWLY.
The striker starts 20 yds from the goal and tries to dribble in order to score.
The goalkeeper moves, reducing the shooting angle and tries to intercept the ball.
Exercises to be carried out facing the goal and on the sides.

Variation   Forward movement of a striker dribbling a FAST ball.

N.B.   The striker must score in a reduced amount of time, maximum five to six seconds (depending on the levels).

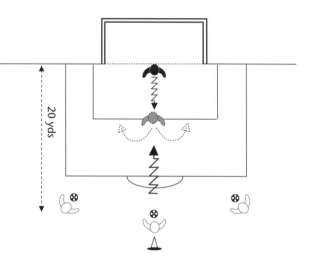

EMPHASIS (points to success)

For the 1st and 2nd situations:
  ✱✱   Combine a well-balanced run-up with a reduction of the shooting angle.
2nd situation:
  ✱✱✱   Avoid too big a stride because the dribbler can change direction.
  ✱✱✱   Stabilize the feet (heels off the ground) at 1.5 yds to 2 yds from the attacker, ready to react to any swerve, then link the striker-goalkeeper tackle.

III TRAINING

Objectives An analysis of specific situations which feature regularly in a match.
Organization In the penalty area and the goal.

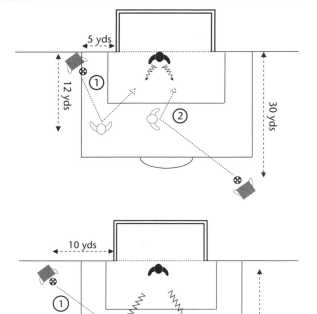

1st situation The goalkeeper is on his line.
The strikers are positioned in the penalty area.
Two servers at some distance from each other; one on the goal line, the other 30 yds from the goal.
When the server passes the ball (starter) the goalkeeper moves forward (reducing the shooting angle), and intercepts after a guided control from the striker.

2nd situation The goalkeeper is positioned on his goal line.
The two strikers are positioned in the 18 yd area.
Two servers at some distance from each other, one near the goal line, the other at 30 yds from the goal.
The server makes a pass between the goalkeeper and the striker (equidistance). The two players move as soon as the ball is kicked (starter) and the goalkeeper intercepts the ball, body shielding, at the feet of the striker.

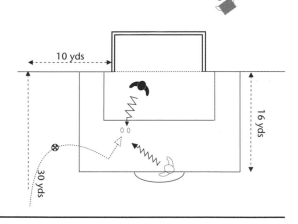

3rd situation The goalkeeper is on his goal line.
A striker is positioned at the 18 yd line.
A server positioned near the middle line hands out high balls.
Tackle: goalkeeper-striker:
After the rebound, the striker tries to shoot or lob at the goalkeeper, who tries to intercept the ball as soon as possible.

EMPHASIS (points to success)

1st situation
✻✻ Anticipate the decision of the striker.
✻✻ Alter your run up depending on the position of the opponent and the ball, then intercede.

2nd situation
✻✻✻ Legs are always bent: Two scenarios are possible:
a) if the goalkeeper gets the ball first: direct interception with the hand.
b) if he comes second on the ball: body shield.
✻✻✻ Assess the judgment of the goalkeeper to work out the correct CHOICE and intercept successfully.

3rd situation
✻✻✻ Any ball which bounces is an advantage for the striker, therefore: the goalkeeper must not commit himself totally but must retain an alternate position either to attack the ball if there is a lack of control on the ball, or move back in case there is an attempt to lob.

THE GAMES

I – INTRODUCTION   II - IMPROVEMENT   III - TRAINING

THE FENCE HOPPER

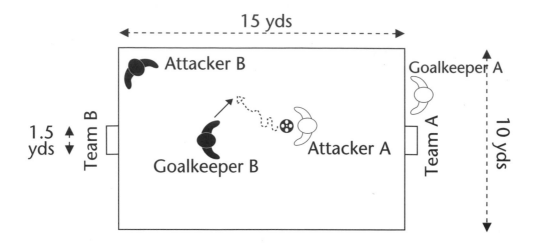

Objective   Carry out as many tackles "striker-goalkeeper" as possible

Organization   A reduced field: length 15 yds; width: 10 yds
(Adapt the area of the field to the level of the players).
Two goals: 1.5 yds wide.
Two teams including a striker and a goalkeeper.

Development   **1st case** •   The striker of team A tries to dribble towards the goalkeeper of
team B in order to score a goal.
The goalkeeper of team B tries to intercede at the feet of
striker "A" in order to intercept the ball.
After having caught the ball, he passes it to striker "B"
who then moves towards goal "A".

   2nd case •   If interceptions are to be carried out, the goals must
be larger because the striker may well shoot faster in
order to score a goal (no tackling).
(Invert the roles (Striker/Goalkeeper) after 10 breaks, 2 x 5).

   Variation   Try to score as many goals as possible in a given time
(faster game).

Count the number of goals scored.

132

CLEARANCE AND DISTRIBUTION

In every match, **the goalkeeper is**, of course, **the last defender**. He is also the **first attacker**.

The **power** and the **accuracy** of his throws and kicks **bring** an **additional tactical component** to his team and enable him to **unbalance** or **counter the opposition**.

Therefore, whatever the pressure set by the opponent or the level of excitement of the goalkeeper, the latter must always be able to **retain** or recover **his clear head-edness** in a short amount of time **in order to carry out his clearance successfully**.

He will therefore be able to use the method **appropriate to each situation** (by hand or foot) at any given time.

However, if the **density** or the **aggressiveness of the opponent do not enable him to master the ball**, he may resort to **clearance with his fists**, in order to drive the danger away.

Lastly, **contemporary soccer focuses** more and more **on the foot skills** of the goal-keeper. **He must therefore possess all the technical knowledge**, take part in all the coaching sessions of the other players and be regularly integrated as field player in the games.

We will therefore study:

THROWS

I INTRODUCTION

Objectives   Break down the movements, giving priority to accuracy, following an exercise carried out over a short distance.

Organization   Vary the distances between the goalkeeper and the receiver of the ball, according to the levels of the players.

1st situation   Two goalkeepers are face to face (10 to 15 yds). They exchange a ball:
a) **Ground rolling passes:** standing, position legs spread one in front of the other, palm of the hand in the direction of the pass, gaining momentum of the throwing arm, backward to forward.
b) **Javelin passes:** like a catapult.
c) **"Rolling-arm" passes:** Arm extended backwards, bring it quickly forward (arc of a circle), legs forward split.
Try to throw to the feet.

2nd situation   Three goalkeepers, positioned in a triangle (10 to 15 yds).
They exchange a ball:
After having blocked the ball, one of the three goalkeepers carries out a ninety-degree turn, then throws it to the next goalkeeper.

Variation   Carry out the exercise taking a "three step" run-up and increase the distance between the goalkeepers.

EMPHASIS (points to success)

✳✳   The movement of the throw is to be synchronized correctly.
✳✳✳   The ball is to produce a descending trajectory (thrown at the feet).
✳✳✳   The hand must always be positioned behind the ball (efficient push).
✳✳✳   Adopt the correct technique with:

Ground rolled passes ⟶ the ball is released at ground level in order to avoid bounces

Javelin passes ⟶ to be used with short throws

Rolled arm passes ⟶ the ball is thrown over the shoulder (avoid side throws)

KICKS

I INTRODUCTION

Objectives   Break down of the movement giving priority to accuracy, following an exercise carried out over a short distance.

Organization   Vary the distance between the goalkeeper and the receiver of the ball, according to the levels of the players.

1st situation   Two goalkeepers are face to face (10 to 15 yds) and exchange a ball:

a) Volley (punt):
The ball is held with both hands, arms extended, supporting leg bent, supporting foot facing the kick, kicking foot backwards and stretched : let go of the ball and kick it just before it touches the ground.

b) Half-volley:
Identical position to the volley, only let the ball fall at the level of the supporting foot and kick it when the supporting foot touches the ground, the kicking foot outstretched.

c) Kick from the ground:
Identical position to the field players: The supporting foot next to the ball or slightly back (in order to vary the trajectories), striking angle 45°, the impact slightly below the center of the ball (in order to lift the ball).

2nd situation   Three goalkeepers are positioned in a triangle (10- 15 yds) and exchange a ball.
After having blocked the ball, one of the three goalkeepers carries out a 90° turn, then kicks the ball to the other goalkeepers.

Variation   Carry out the exercise taking a "three step" run up and increase the distance between the goalkeepers.

EMPHASIS (points to success)

✳✳✳   For punts and half volleys, at a standstill: lay the ball down in front of you (slightly forward after the run up) keeping the arms extended.

✳✳✳   In order to obtain a straight trajectory of the ball, it must be kicked in its center.
   • If the kick is sideways (often with the outside of the foot) = curved trajectory
   • If the kick is too high ——► the foot is placed under the ball and either kicked too early for the volleys, or too late after the rebound for the half volleys.

II IMPROVEMENT

Common Situations
(Vary the distance between goalkeeper and partner)

Objectives Link an outlet pass adapted to the situation of the game with a run up and catch.

Organization In a goal and a half field.

1st situation The server kicks the ball at the goalkeeper (vary the kicks).
The goalkeeper catches the ball and throws it back to the opposite side, aiming at a target.
Exercise to be carried out right then left, varying the distance between the goalkeeper and the target (20 to 30 yds).

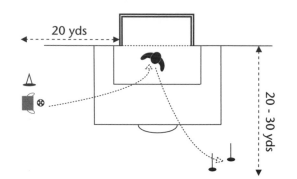

2nd situation Throw with varying trajectories.
The goalkeeper catches the ball then throws it back to a moving partner.
Exercise to be carried out right then left, varying the distance between goalkeeper and partner (20 to 30 yds).

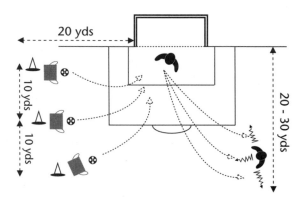

EMPHASIS (points to success)

✳✳✳ Look for a clearance in a free space and in the direction of the run of the partner (call for the ball).

✳✳✳ Avoid throwing back on the main line.

✳✳✳ Make the outlet pass to the opposite side to the source of the ball (starting point).

III TRAINING

Common Situations

Objectives Outlet under pressure. It is possible to include an opponent acting as a shield.

Organization Use the goal and half of the field.

1st situation Combine speed and precision.
Begin on the goal line.
The goalkeeper makes the outlet passes, returning each time to the goal line.
Each ball must pass through a gate (set the choice of the gate).
Exercises to be carried out with the hand then with the foot.

Variation Replace the gates with moving partners.

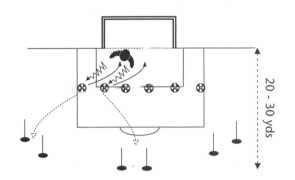

2nd situation Two servers of the ball.
An opponent at a standstill in front of the goalkeeper.
A partner who recovers the ball. (call-marking).
An opponent marking the partner.
The goalkeeper recovers the ball distributed by a server and throws it back at the moving partner (call for the ball).

Vary the length, short and long, of the hand and foot clearances.

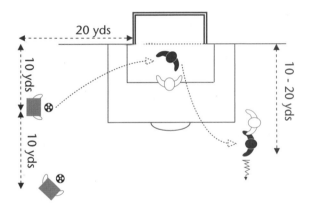

EMPHASIS (points to success)

* ✳✳ Try to clear in the direction of the run of the partner.
* ✳✳ Remain clear headed in the choice of the clearance (opposite side to the source of the ball, by hand or foot).

FOOT TECHNIQUE OF THE FIELD PLAYERS ADAPTED TO THE CLEARANCE OF THE GOALKEEPER

I INTRODUCTION

Objectives   The move is carried out at a slow pace and over short distances. Aim for accuracy.

Organization   Use a wire netting, 10 to 15 yds high; facing the goalkeeper, if possible.

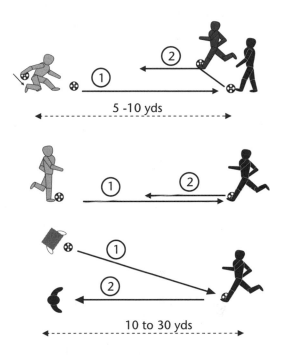

1st situation   The server and the goalkeeper are facing each other (5 to 10 yds apart).
After a hand pass, then a foot pass by the server, the goalkeeper kicks the ball
1) – after having stopped the ball - over the server
2) – without stopping the ball - over the server

Variation   a) – the server throws balls with various effects (lifted, deflected, with a bounce).
b) – Position a non-moving partner at a distance between 10-30 yds from the goalkeeper, first at a stand still then introduce movement in order to recover the ball.

2nd situation   On a side pass (right then left) made by the server, the goalkeeper throws the ball back to a partner positioned in front of him (vary the distance between goalkeepers and partner by 10 yds to 30 yds).

3rd situation   On a slow kick made by a server, straight on then from the side, the goalkeeper runs and kicks the ball on the main line or on the sides, towards a close then a distant partner.

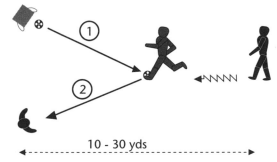

EMPHASIS (points to success)

✳✳   Adapt the kicking technique of the field player to the situation (position of the supporting foot-kicking foot).

✳✳✳   Try to lift the ball on the clearance (supporting foot behind the ball when kicking).

✳✳✳   Clear with accuracy in all circumstances.

✳✳   Dribble as field players regularly do (right foot left foot).

II IMPROVEMENT

Objectives Carry out the movement despite moderate opposition.

Organization Use the penalty area.

1st situation The goalkeeper is positioned 9 yds from the goal.
A partner dribbles the ball and pushes it towards the goal-keeper at the edge of the penalty area (1).
The goalkeeper triggers his run when the ball is pushed by the partner and clears it (2).

2 possibilities a) Long clearance (look for the wings)
b) Short clearance to the right or left.
In all cases, a striker puts pressure on the goalkeeper.
The partner begins his move on the central line and on the wings.

2nd situation The organization is identical to the first situation, only the ball is thrown by a server situated between the striker and the goalkeeper.
• The server sends the ball on the central line or on the sides.
• Tackle goalkeeper/striker on the central line or on the wings.

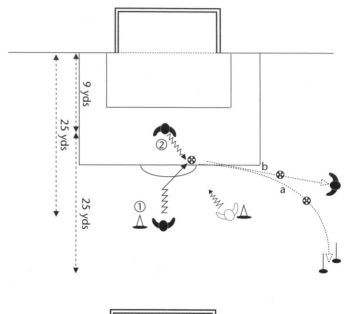

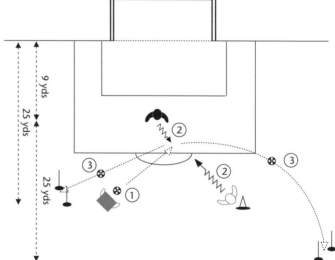

EMPHASIS (points to success)

✳✳✳ Pay careful attention to the ball when kicked (study the trajectory).

✳✳ Link the run and the clearance well.

✳✳ Remain clear headed in spite of the presence of opposition.

III TRAINING

Objectives Carry out the movement as in a real game including dynamic opposition.

Organization Use the goal and the penalty area.

1st situation The goalkeeper is 9 yds from the goal.
Two strikers are positioned at the angles of the penalty area. The server throws to one of the two strikers (your choice). As soon as the pass has been made, tackle between goalkeeper and striker.
Aim of the goalkeeper: outlet to a target situated 20 yds from the goal.
Aim of the striker: try to score.

2nd situation The goalkeeper is in the 6 yd area (alone).
Two defenders against two strikers between the 6 yd line and the 18 yd line.
• the defenders, after a minimum of two passes, slide the ball towards their goalkeeper, in order for him to score in one of the two targets.
• the strikers only try to intercept the pass made by the defender to the goalkeeper in order to score (under pressure).

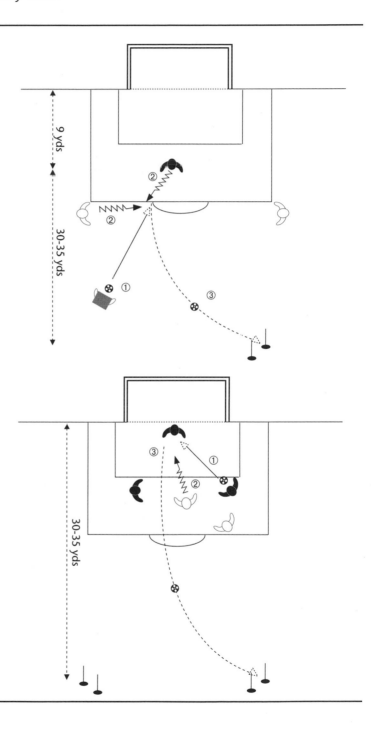

EMPHASIS (points to success)

✳✳✳ Keep calm in all circumstances.
✳✳ High reaction speed is necessary.
Important: In short games, include the goalkeeper as a field player in order to improve his foot technique.

CLEARANCE WITH THE FIST

I INTRODUCTION

Objectives   Ambidextrous handling of the ball (right fist, then left fist).
Improve the skill of the goalkeeper.
Organization Try to use a wall.

1st situation   Individual juggling of the goalkeeper.
• With one fist (right then left).
• Alternate both fists (right-left-right…).
• With both fists ; alternate hits.
Try to elevate the ball higher and higher.

2nd situation   Juggling against a wall (see 1st situation for the different options).

3rd situation   Two goalkeepers are facing each other at 5 yds and exchange balls using one or both fists.

4th situation   Exchange between three goalkeepers positioned in a triangle.
Catching the ball on one side and fisting it on the other.
Use only one fist (right then left).

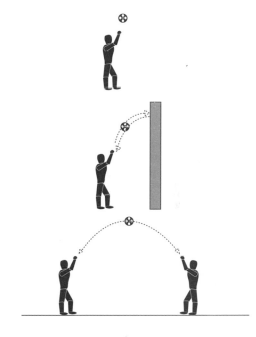

EMPHASIS (points to success)

✳✳✳   Carry out the exercise, emphasizing the quality of the move.
a) Accurate contact ⟶ tight fist (avoid the joints).
b) The wrist is the extension of the forearm (no bent wrist).
c) Hit the ball in its center (quick and accurate move).

✳✳✳   In order to hit with both fists:
The fists are facing each other (fingers to fingers for a larger contact area) and elbows to the body.

✳✳✳   Do not hit the ball if it is too low (below the eyes).

II IMPROVEMENT

Objectives   A combination of moves followed by a clearance ; include an opponent (moderate opposition).

Organization Use a goal area and the 6 yd area.

1st situation The goalkeeper intervenes with both fists on a ball thrown high above the head of a striker positioned in front of him.
Outlet towards the server.

2nd situation A goalkeeper in his goal.
An opponent at 6 yds.
An off-centered server (right then left) carries out a high center pass towards the head of the striker. Interception by the goalkeeper who clears with a fist towards a target situated at the opposite side of the source of the ball.

3rd situation Identical to the second situation, but a ball is thrown from in front; clearance with both fists high and far towards a gate, situated slightly on the main line.

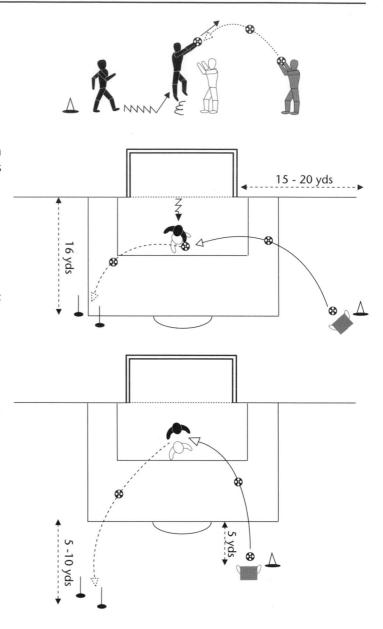

EMPHASIS (points to success)

✳✳✳   To clear with one fist:
On a ball coming from the right ⟶ clear with the right fist towards the left.
On a ball coming from the left ⟶ clear with the left fist towards the right.

✳✳✳   To clear with both fists:
On a high, frontal ball, the goalkeeper punches the ball far (the ball must pass over the head of the opposite striker).

III TRAINING

Objectives   Disrupted tackles and movements in a real game situation with a high DENSITY of players (partners/opponents) in front of the goal.

Organization Use half a field.

1st situation   Tackle goalkeeper/goalkeeper (2).
The server throws a high ball.
Equal distance between both goal-keepers.
After the ball has been thrown (starter) the goalkeepers run and intercept with the fist (possible shoulder to shoulder contact).

N.B.   The run is disrupted by cones placed on the ground.

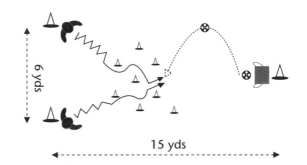

2nd situation   Servers are positioned on the wings or in the center.
Partners and opponents are in a given area in front of the goal.
The goalkeeper intercedes despite field players (partners and opponents) who play the ball on the main line and on the wings.
The ball is cleared towards different targets.
Vary the position of the servers.

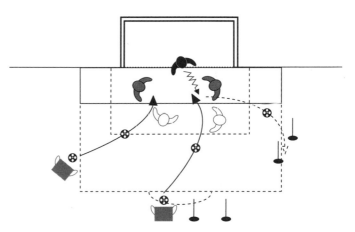

EMPHASIS (points to success)

✳✳✳   Use the clearance with the fist only if absolutely necessary *(do not neglect the catch of the ball if it is possible)*.

✳✳✳   Use the command for the goalkeeper.

✳✳   Choose well (one or both fists) depending on the situation.

THE GAMES

I – INTRODUCTION   II - IMPROVEMENT   III - TRAINING

THE FENCE HOPPER

Objective
Combine precision with power in the clearance in order to unbalance the opposite team searching for empty spaces.

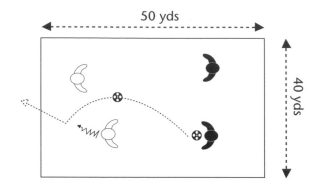

Organization
Use the width of half a field (50 yds by 40 yds), or the length of a field, depending on the level of the players and the choice of the clearance. i.e.:
• Fist (s) and ground clearance, ball stopped (6 yds) ⟶ half a field.
• Half volley, volley and moving ball on the ground ⟶ a whole field

Development
Try to score, bringing the ball behind the goal line of the opposite team.
After having studied the trajectory of the opposite clearance, the goalkeeper may either :
    1- clear at the falling point or
    2- pass to a partner positioned at his level or behind him.
    If the ball goes out of bounds ⟶ put the ball back into play by clearing
    If a goal is scored ⟶ engagement at 10 or 20 yds from his goal line (depending on the level of the players).

VOLLEYBALL

(Clearance with the fist)

Objective
Use one or both fists in an aerial tackle.

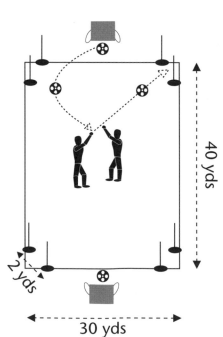

Organization
Two goalkeepers against each other in a set area.
(30 by 40 yds improvement level).
Adapt the size of the game area depending on the levels of the players.
Each has two goals to attack and two goals to defend.

Development
Each goalkeeper tries to score a point by clearing the ball into one of the two targets situated in front of him.
The server varies the height of the balls (throw then kick).

CONCLUSION

Whether the coach is a goalkeeper or not, and **regardless of his experiences,** he should be able to base his teaching upon the general principles which have been outlined in this book.

It is your task, therefore, to promote in your goalkeeper his own individualism once he has absorbed the basics.

In **order to reach these targets,** you will then need to act as an **enlightened advisor** and **not as a coach, callous to all expressions of an innate talent.**

The **role of the goalkeeper** is such a **vast subject** that it cannot be dealt with **in one book.**

Principally, it was our aim to address two essential themes: the Physical Preparation and the Technique. Inevitably, certain other areas have been omitted which remain to be developed.

To quote but a few:
- The PSYCHOLOGICAL ASPECTS of the goalkeeper,
- The TACTICAL APPROACH and the STOPPED KICKS,
- The ACROBATIC MOVEMENTS and SPECIFIC STRENGTH TRAINING,
- The WARM-UP of the Goalkeeper,
- PLANNING the COACHING ,

Etc…etc…

CONTENTS

TECHNICAL PREPARATION

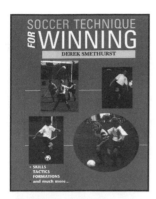

#155 Soccer Technique for Winning
by Derek Smethurst
$14.95

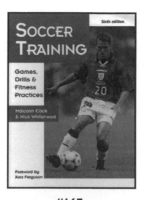

**#167
Soccer Training
Games, Drills, and
Fitness Exercises**
by Malcolm Cook
$14.95

**#169
Coaching Advanced
Players**
by Richard Bate
$12.95

**#785
The Complete Book of
Soccer Restart Plays**
by Pereni and Bonfanti
$14.95

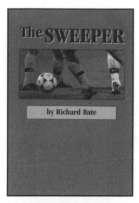

#225 The Sweeper
by Richard Bate
$9.95

**#792 120 Competitive
Games and Exercises
For Soccer**
by Nicola Pica
$14.95

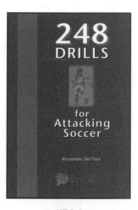

**#794
248 Drills for
Attacking Soccer**
by Alessandro Del Freo
$14.95

**#787
Attacking Schemes
and Training
Exercises**
by Fascetti and Scaia
$14.95

**#265
Coordination, Agility and
Speed Training for Soccer**
by Peter Schreiner
$14.95

**#266
24 Easy to Follow
Training Sessions
for 5-7 Year Olds**
by Peter Schreiner
$12.95

**#297
24 Easy to Follow
Practice Sessions
for 8-11 Year Olds**
by Peter Schreiner
$12.95

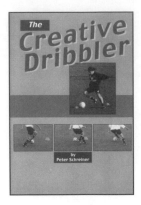

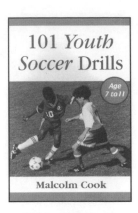

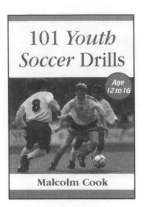

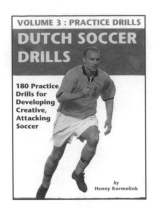

**#256 The Creative
Dribbler**
by Peter Schreiner
$14.95

**#254   101 Youth
Soccer Drills
Ages 7-11**
by Malcolm Cook
$14.95

**#255   101 Youth
Soccer Drills
Ages 12-16**
by Malcolm Cook
$14.95

**#195
Dutch Soccer Drills Vol. 3**
by Henny Kormelink
$12.95

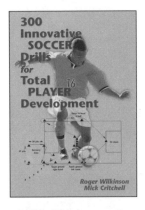

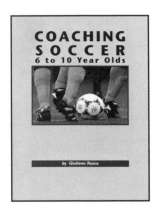

**#188 300 Innovative
SOCCER Drills for Total
PLAYER Development**
*by Roger Wilkinson
and Mick Critchell*
$14.95

**#264 Coaching Soccer
6 to 10 year Olds**
by Giuliano Rusca
$14.95

**#149 Soccer Tactics
An Analysis of Attack
and Defense**
by Massimo Lucchesi
$12.95

**#249 Coaching the
3-4-3**
by Massimo Lucchesi
$12.95

**#161 Goalkeeping
Drills
Volume One**
*by
Gerd Thissen
Klaus Röllgen*
$12.95

**#162 Goalkeeping
Drills
Volume Two**
*by
Gerd Thissen
Klaus Röllgen*
$12.95

DATE DUE

GAYLORD		PRINTED IN U.S.A.